THE SHEFFIELD FLOOD
March 11th 1864

By
Peter Machan

Illustrated by Eric Leslie

© Peter Machan 1999

Printed and published by:
ALD Design & Print
279 Sharrow Vale Road
Sheffield S11 8ZF

Telephone 0114 268 6269
E:mail ald@printshop.demon.co.uk

ISBN 1-901587-05-3

First Published 1999

Other titles in the series:

Mi-Amigo - The Story of Sheffield's Flying Fortress - David Harvey	ISBN 1-901587-00-2
Tales From a Peak District Bookshop - Mike Smith	ISBN 1-901587-01-0
Tha' Don't look Proper - Anne Hunt	ISBN 1-901587-02-9
Shiny Sheff - The Story of Sheffield's Fighting Ships - Alistair Lofthouse	ISBN 1-901587-03-7
Doug's War - An Erksome Business - Doug Sanderson	ISBN 1-901587-04-5
Carl Wark - Peak District Fortress or Folly ? - Mick Savage	ISBN 1-901587 06-1

Contents

Acknowledgements

Thanks for help and support in producing this book go to:-

Tom Sharp and Pegasus Theatre for the original idea and encouragement.

J. France for the copies of photographs which he made from his set of stereoscope pictures of the flood.

Mary Machan for her assistance with the proof reading.

Staff at Sheffield Local Studies library and Kelham Island Museum for access to their extensive collections of photographs and artefacts.

And finally:-

To Eric Leslie for his inspired illustrations, without which this book would not have been possible.

For Jenny and Adam

The Author

All aspects of local history have long held an interest for Peter Machan. He is a well-known speaker on local topics, and has often led walks and trails which recreate the City's past.

It was as headteacher of Malin Bridge Junior School, however, that he developed a particular fascination for the story of the Sheffield Flood, as descendants of the families whose names tragically appear in the list of those lost still attended the school.

His previous publications include:-

Water Mills of the River Sheaf (1975)
Models of Sheffield Trams (1979)
Pictorial Map of Historical Sheffield (1983)
Made in Sheffield (1985)
John Watts; 200 Years of a Sheffield Cutler, in *Aspects of Sheffield II* (1999)

Peter is presently headteacher at Bankwood Primary School in the Gleadless Valley.

*   *   *   *   *   *   *   *   *   *

Although Eric Leslie now lives in exile in North Devon, he has impeccable roots, being born and brought up in the Loxley Valley. He attended Malin Bridge School as a boy. Eric is a well-known writer, artist and illustrator and his publications include :-

The Leek and Manifold Light Railway (1976)
Trams, Tiddlers and Tizer (1989)
Oatcakes, Pikelets and Sarsparilla (1991)
A Backward Glance (1993)

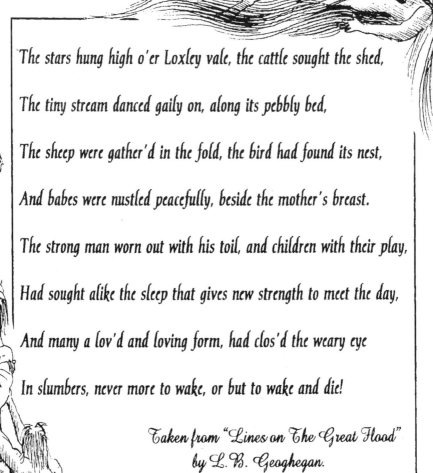

The stars hung high o'er Loxley vale, the cattle sought the shed,

The tiny stream danced gaily on, along its pebbly bed,

The sheep were gather'd in the fold, the bird had found its nest,

And babes were nustled peacefully, beside the mother's breast.

The strong man worn out with his toil, and children with their play,

Had sought alike the sleep that gives new strength to meet the day,

And many a lov'd and loving form, had clos'd the weary eye

In slumbers, never more to wake, or but to wake and die!

> Taken from "Lines on The Great Flood"
> by L. B. Geoghegan.

A Very Local Disaster

To several generations of Sheffield people the disaster which struck the town at midnight on March 11th 1864, when the Dale Dyke Dam collapsed, allowing the waters of its reservoir to burst down the Loxley Valley, has simply been known as 'T'Flood'. To those few from outside the locality who have ever heard of the terrible events of that night, when some two hundred and fifty people were killed, it is known as 'The Sheffield Flood', but these are now few indeed for the disaster, whose death toll was to mark it out as the greatest calamity of Victorian England, was of passing interest to the country in general. This was a local event, but it was not of purely local significance. The tumult caused as the flood swept down the valley that dismal night disturbed more than the bed of the river. It stirred the mud of mid-Victorian society, revealing its poverty, squalor and shame. The story itself is deservedly a local favourite, for it combines all the elements of the best drama; suspense, grief, courage and comedy. Only later came the elements of recrimination, hypocrisy and downright dishonesty.

By any standards this disaster was of international proportions and it is to be hoped that its annual entry in the Guinness Book of Records as 'The Worst British Dam Burst Disaster' will never be superceded. The flood did evince some immediate national interest, although the London press reported the happenings as though they had taken place in a distant colony, expending more words on minute descriptions of the local scenery than on compassionate reporting of the suffering of the victims and survivors. For a few weeks in the spring of 1864 the spotlight of Victorian sensationalism was focussed on the Loxley Valley. Indeed, Queen Victoria herself, no great lover of the filthy town of Sheffield, sent not only her condolences but also a personal contribution to the relief fund. The newly-constructed railways advertised 'excursion specials' which brought sightseers from far and wide to view the scene of the disaster. But once the visiting hoards of trippers to the scene of the wrecked dam wall and the publishers of doggerel had satisfied that mawkish Victorian fascination with death, the story was all but erased from national consciousness and sank to the level of local folklore.

This was not the only disaster of any note to strike the country during the nineteenth century. Most people's minds will immediately recall the dreadful story of the Tay Bridge Disaster in 1879, which, unlike the Sheffield Flood, caused a national outcry and entered the history books, despite its far smaller death toll. It is probably not entirely cynical to suppose that the reason for this seemingly strange historical twist lies in the fact that the victims of Sheffield's tragedy came from the poorer classes. The property qualifications to vote ensured that the poor were unrepresented in Parliament and therefore the town's two Members put no pressure on the Home Secretary to establish a Commission of Inquiry. They knew that their best interests lay in serving the interests of the middle class voters who were likely to own shares in the Water Company.

Contemporary accounts of this story provide us with a unique snapshot of the intimate details of the lives of those ordinary persons about which history records so little. These few days in March 1864 are undoubtedly the most intensively recorded in Sheffield's long history but, had it not been for the skill and determination of a local reporter, even the names of those poor families of cottagers swept to their deaths would be difficult to trace. The man to whom they owe their singularly compelling epitaph is Samuel Harrison, the successful publisher of the weekly *Sheffield Times*. It was he who followed up and recorded with dogged determination the many human interest stories connected with the night's events and welded them into a fascinating chronology of the disaster. In his book, he compiled eye-witness accounts and reports of subsequent investigations, inquests and relief measures as well as tables showing the details of the dead and missing and of damage to property. Through these accounts Harrison presents us with one of the few systematic eye-witness descriptions of the living conditions of the poor in Sheffield in the mid-nineteenth century. The picture he paints is of a town which is unfamiliar today, even though we recognise and can trace many of the streets and locations struck by the disaster. In the Dickensian town he portrays, people sleep in boxes at their workplace or in sheds, sharing their crowded town centre yards with cowsheds, pigsties and stables. Parents leave their sleeping family of young children to walk miles at night gathering watercress, whilst others follow occupations described as 'manglewoman', 'shuttleman' or 'toll collector'. Without Harrison's account we would simply be left with the stark records from inquests and inquiries. What we actually have is infinitely more evocative. He deserves to be remembered as well as the disaster he recorded so vividly. Harrison's book was published as 'A Complete History of the Great Flood at Sheffield'. Its style is as compelling and immediate as it was when it was written, over one hundred and thirty years ago. Much of what follows is simply a retelling of the story using the facts collected by Harrison. A tasteful stone memorial to Samuel Harrison, who died at the early age of 44 in 1871, stands near the gates of the Victorian General Cemetery. It bears no mention of his most memorable contribution to posterity.

The Power of Water

Long before this time, Sheffield had made a fine reputation for the production of the highest quality steel products, especially edge tools of all kinds, and the mills in which men worked to forge and grind the blades were still strung out like beads along the streams which tumble down deep valleys from the Pennine uplands to the west. Their water-powered wheels had turned since Tudor times, and would continue to turn long into the age of steam. Water was a vital resource without which the local economy would never have developed, so there was perhaps a certain irony in this tragedy having struck through the first ill-judged efforts to augment the natural supply to the mill owners, for the purpose of the construction of the Dale Dyke reservoir had been to provide a constant flow down the Loxley Valley to ensure that the wheels kept turning. When complete, four new dams, Dale Dyke, Agden, Strines and Damflask were to provide a much needed supply of fresh water piped to the squalid back streets of the town beyond. In the event, the crashing waters were to obliterate every mill in the valley.

The Loxley Valley, the most northerly of the tributaries which join the Don in Sheffield, was similar to the others which reached into the Pennine moorlands to the west. The waters of its stream were used and reused again and again as they tumbled over twenty six water wheels, powering a variety of mills in its six mile length. As well as the forges and grinding wheels, here were corn mills, paper mills, wire-drawing mills and a mill where glass was ground. The grinding wheels were known locally as 'hulls', a Yorkshire term which harks back to their rural, semi-agricultural nature. In these hulls the grinders toiled, pressing the blades forged in local hearths, against the spinning grindstones, daily shortening their lives as they breathed the deadly cocktail of dust which would inevitably lead to a premature death from 'grinders' disease'.

The inhabitants of a town situated on a network of rivers suffered particularly harshly from the lack of a supply of clean water. In earlier days, until well into the eighteenth century, there had been a number of wells and springs to meet their needs. The Barker's Pool in the town centre was the best known of these, although towards the end of the eighteenth century, it was used only to release water to flush the streets. It was removed as a nuisance, and not before time if the lines that a local poet wrote of it were true;

> 'The Barker's Pool, noted for nuisance indeed,
> Green over with venom where insects did breed'.

There are earlier records of the pool being used for quite different purposes when the 'cuck stool' was occasionally brought here from its usual position at Lady's Bridge, and the prospect of being dunked into such a foetid tank must have served as the strongest discouragement to prospective nagging Sheffield wives! But such days were beyond memory. New sources of water were built to supply the needs of the growing number of people in the rapidly developing town, and not before time, for the town's dynamic expansion in the earliest years of the nineteenth century

3

'This vast work stretched itself across the valley for the space of 400 yards.

In the embankment, there were about 400,000 cubic yards of material.

The weir that was provided to carry off the overflow was 60 feet wide.'

Samuel Harrison

4

entirely outstripped its former resources. Even after a series of ten new reservoirs had been constructed on Crookes Moor, overlooking the town, between 1782 and 1830, a constant supply was still only ensured to the wealthy in the affluent houses stretching up the hillsides. The occupiers of the town centre courtyards could still only rely on an intermittent supply from communal pumps and taps. Since this had to be stored for long periods in tubs or barrels the risk of infection was acute, especially as sanitation was primitive in the extreme. Disease was rife in the town. Malaria, typhus and cholera were all endemic diseases which were a direct result of an inadequate clean water supply. In 1832 a major outbreak of cholera struck the inhabitants of the lower parts of town, especially around Pond Street. Just over four hundred townspeople lie buried in a communal burial place on the hillside overlooking the station.

So much water was being extracted from the rivers by the many mills and manufacturers that even the Don was reduced to a slimy brown trickle, the stench of which drifted under the noses of even those responsible for the administration of the growing town, the Town Trustees and the Council. It is unthinkable to imagine what would have happened if The Sheffield Waterworks Company had not been incorporated in 1830 and set about with a will to remedy the worsening situation. Even so the inhabitants of the poorer parts of the town were to see little real improvement for many years to come, since all that the company could manage to do was to try to keep pace with the continuing massive increase in demand.

In the thirty four years since its incorporation the company had built three new reservoirs at Redmires on the Wyming Brook on the western fringe of Sheffield, and by 1848 had completed the two reservoirs in the Rivelin Valley, mainly to provide compensation water. With this the company proclaimed itself well able to provide for any foreseeable demands. It came as something of a surprise to them, therefore, that in only five years they were planning the huge 'Bradfield Scheme' of three new reservoirs, Dale Dyke, Agden and Strines in the upper reaches of the Loxley Valley. Surely now, the company felt, once this grand scheme was in place, Sheffield would have a water supply to meet all its needs which would be the envy of many another industrial town. It had been in this spirit of civic pride, optimism and confidence that the excavations for the embankment at Dale Dyke were begun on 1st January, 1859.

Visitors to the site during the five years of the construction were awestruck by the massive scale of operations. Although it was designed on the same principles which had proved their worth in similar projects all over the world, no similar works of civil engineering had been witnessed locally. The vast wall, which stretched a quarter of a mile across the valley floor, gradually grew to its full height of a hundred feet as armies of navvies toiled with donkey carts, barrows and trucks on rails. The embankment was triangular in section, with a massive base five hundred feet wide tapering to twelve feet at the top. At the centre of this was the puddled clay wall which was to act as a waterproof membrane. It was on the integrity of this that the capacity of the dam to hold water would depend. This was exacting work for, as the puddle clay wall was being constructed, layers of finely-graded material had to be built up on either side and compacted in thicknesses of no more than six feet at a time. Great care had to be taken to ensure that stones did not fall into the puddle wall which was being built up some ten feet below. The scene was one of constant activity. The top-hatted resident engineer, John Gunson, interpreted the plans drawn up by the company's consulting engineer, John Towlerton Leather and directed the contractors, Messrs. Craven, Cockayne and Fountain, who in turn supervised the armies of navvies. Many of these labourers had been recruited locally but others had spent their whole working life trekking from one of the many railway construction sites to the next.

Now, after five years, the work on Dale Dyke was virtually complete.

Summoned to the Dam

At 8.30 p.m. on the evening of that fateful March day in 1864, Charlotte Gunson waved goodbye to her husband John, from the cosy parlour window of their town house at number 14 Division Street. John Gunson pulled his cloak around himself, against the rain which bounced off the cobbles, far too preoccupied with his thoughts about the message that he had just received to think to look back. He greeted John Craven, one of his contractors, and together they climbed into the gig to drive out to the wild site of the Dale Dyke Dam on the edge of the Derbyshire moors. "Poor John," she thought as she turned from the window, "dragged out yet again in this awful weather!" She knew there was no question of him refusing to travel the eight miles to the dam for the second time that day. Her husband had a clear sense of duty, and there could be no doubt, his was a huge responsibility.

It is not difficult to imagine what thoughts were going through John Gunson's mind as the wheels of his gig rattled along the cobblestone roads of Sheffield towards the village of Hillsborough, the horse and gig buffeted by biting wind and slanting rain making conversation impossible. It was a road he knew well for, as the resident engineer of the Sheffield Waterworks Company, John Gunson had to supervise the contractors who employed the men to prepare the ground and construct the huge embankment across Bradfield Dale at the head of the Loxley Valley. He and Craven had travelled the eight mile route countless times since excavations were started. As the gig rattled past the newly-built barracks, rowdy groups of soldiers in bright dress uniform made their way across to The Queens Hotel. He acknowledged the friendly wave of Thomas Winter, the seventy-year-old keeper of the toll house beside Hillsborough Bridge, one of the few who, recognising the engineer, would be left only until midnight to ponder the reason for such a late journey. Mr. Gunson shivered and pulled his dark cloak and waterproof cape more tightly around him. After all, he was no longer a young man. By hard work and loyal service over the previous thirty years he had risen within the company until, now well into his fifties, he occupied the resident engineer's house, next door to the Company offices in Division Street.

All was now entirely dark, the last dim, comforting lights showing from the few unshuttered windows having been left behind. The gig set the local dogs barking, clattering through the collection of houses and pubs clustered around the corn mill where the Rivelin meets the Loxley at Malin Bridge. Gunson was apprehensive. He had been concerned enough about the weather after reading the warnings of a gale in the Times Newspaper to alter his plan to inspect the Redmires Reservoir and travel to Dale Dyke earlier the same day. Had concerns regarding the safety of that massive bank already entered his head? Was it a nagging doubt arising from the peculiar difficulties that the engineer had encountered during the past three years of the dam's construction or was it simply a reflection of his natural caution and anticipation of possible problems following the ferocious weather conditions of the past weeks?

The summons which had drawn John Gunson so abruptly from his comfortable parlour fireside had been delivered just after eight. At first he hadn't recognised young Stephenson Fountain, the son of one of the subcontractors at the dam, as the maid led him awkwardly into the over-furnished room. The lad was out of breath, soaking wet and windblown but this was only too understandable since he had just ridden eight miles from the construction site in the Loxley Valley to bring a message from his father. He stood in the doorway, awkwardly twisting his hat between his hands, aware of the drips forming a small puddle on the plush carpet. Never in all his life had Stephenson felt so uncomfortable. The contrast between the numbing cold and wet, through which he had ridden for the last hour, and the closeness of the small sitting room, together with the effects of exhaustion, quickly brought a bright flush to his face and made his head start to swim. Only very rarely had he visited the town of Sheffield, and he had never before had reason to call on the chief engineer in his own home.

John Gunson felt some of the boy's discomfort. He was, however, far too anxious to hear what pressing news could have brought the lad on such an unaccustomed errand to think to invite him to sit. Instead he sprang to his feet, letting drop the copy of The Times newspaper in which he had been rereading the latest bulletin on the weather written by Captain Fitzroy. He found that these forecasts, compiled by the famous sea captain, were generally to be relied upon and today's outlook gave him little comfort. The weather continued to be dominated by low pressure to the east, bringing rain-sodden winds sweeping from the west across the high Pennine moorlands. The new Dale Dyke Dam was filling at an alarming rate and the water was pounding against the newly-built wall.

"I'm sorry to trouble you Mr. Gunson, sir, but my father says to tell you that they've found a crack in the embankment", explained the young messenger. "It were William Horsefield, one of father's men, that noticed it shortly after you left at about half past five. It's probably nothing to worry about, father thinks. It's just a minor settlement crack, or it might just be the frost. I hope that you'll excuse me disturbing you on such a night, but the men thought that you'd want to know about it." "Tell me, have you seen this crack yourself, Stephenson?" asked the engineer, his concern clearly apparent at hearing the most unwelcome news imaginable."Yes sir, I went up there after George Swinden sent for father." "And what does this

'William Horsefield, as he proceeded along, noticed a crack in the side of the embankment. Mr. Fountain sent his son, Stephenson, to tell Mr. Gunson to come to the reservoir as soon as possible.'

Samuel Harrison

crack look like then?" "I wouldn't say it were wide, Mr. Gunson, but it's quite long. It runs for about fifty yards along the embankment, about twelve foot from t'top." "I'd better see for myself. Is anyone else there?" "Aye, you know how word gets round between workmen and farmers. By the time I left at about seven o'clock there were around, oh I'd say, two dozen. Mr. Ibbotson were there, from t'corn mill at Bradfield, with his brothers, and t'school teacher, Mr. Nicholls. Mr. Swinden's telling 'em all that there's no danger but Richard Ibbotson keeps worrying everybody wi' talk of a dream that his wife had last night about his house being flooded." "You say you left Bradfield at seven, Stephenson? How did it take you so long to get here?" "I'm sorry sir, but it weren't my fault. My horse's saddle girth broke when I were going through Damflask. I had to lead the horse to the Barrel Inn. I knew that Jonathan Ibbotson would be able to mend it. He were surprised to see me too, on a night like this. I had to tell him about the crack and that I was on my way to Sheffield to fetch you, Mr. Gunson. I hope I didn't do wrong sir?" "So do I young man, but it can't be helped now. I can see that I'd better make all speed."

Charlotte, his wife was flustered at having the domestic arrangements so abruptly disturbed as well as deeply concerned at the thought of her husband setting off once more into such a wild night."Surely," she said "there are others up at Dale Dyke who can deal with the situation without you having to go all that way on a night like this. You've done enough today. You will catch your death of cold. "But her entreaties were futile and from long experience of her husband she had been well aware of this from the start. "Don't you worry now my dear. You know that it's my place to go and see that all's well with the dam. You get on to bed," and he was already pulling on his heaviest cloak and hat from the wooden stand in the narrow hallway. "Mary, have the boy bring the gig round while I go and collect Mr. Craven to accompany me." Tapping the ornate barometer beside the coat stand in the hall, he quickly went out into the cold and wet, aware that he had a long night ahead of him, but mercifully yet unaware of the horrors that it would unleash.

The two men had soon climbed into the gig and the driver, perched behind them, urged the unwilling horse down Balm Green past the pump which was all that remained to show where the Barker's Pool, the earliest town water supply, had stood for hundreds of years. Even on a night like this the narrow Fargate and High Street were alive with end of the week revellers, spilling from the noisy public houses on either side, more of them in the rough working clothes worn by the grinders and other cutlery workers than in the now fashionable ladies' crinolines and men's tall hats, but all of them drawing their outer clothes tightly around themselves and hurrying against the cold and wind. As they turned at the market place to go down Angel Street the two men remarked on the lurid glow from the newly-extended furnaces at the massive Atlas steel works of John Brown which lit up the night sky above the Don Valley, indicating that the great cauldrons of bubbling steel, recently installed to the pattern of Henry Bessemer, were showering their impressive pyrotechnics into the night sky. Tonight the gusting wind carried away the rumbling and the metallic thumping which had disturbed the sleep of the people of the town for the last few years, as the steam engines in the new steel mills along the Don Valley to the east of the town rolled and hammered anything from railway lines to armour plating. Tonight even the great plumes of

'Overcrowding and insanitary conditions of all kinds abound in the slums, and back-to-back houses are common. The water supply is very inadequate, one tap often being the sole supply for a large number of houses.'

B.S. Rowntree

filthy smoke issuing as usual from the forest of chimneys which grew at varying heights from every cutlery works and steel mill in the town and out along the valleys was being blown in tattered streaks to darken the buildings in Rotherham and Doncaster for a change.

Down the steep Snig Hill the road became almost blocked, the vendors shouting their wares and shopkeepers doing brisk business from the rundown wooden framed shops which jutted into the road. It wasn't until the gig turned into West Bar, as the road swung left in front of The Packhorse Inn, that it could pick up its pace. The crowds here were even noisier, anticipating a raucous evening's entertainment at the Bijou Theatre's second house of the night, and it was only with difficulty above the rattle of the wheels on the cobbles and the carousing that Mr. Gunson was able to make himself heard as he familiarised Mr. Craven, the contractor, with what he understood to be the situation at the newly-completed dam. "But you were at the dam yourself only this afternoon weren't you Mr. Gunson? Surely you'd have seen if there were owt amiss." "Yes, I spent most of the day up there, although I'd intended to go up to Redmires as you know." "Was it the weather made you change your mind?" "Well, now that we are so near to having everything finished I must keep a close watch on how things are proceeding. The level of the water is well up, only about eighteen inches below the level of the overflow weir this afternoon, and still filling. We can't be too careful now can we?" "But what could go wrong now? If there's a slight crack in t'embankment it'll only be settlin' a bit. It'll do that for months until all t'layers of material have consolidated." "You may well be right. I do hope so. I saw nothing to concern me today I must say, but the sight of that great sheet of water being licked into spray against the dam wall that we built just made me stop and think again." "Made you think what, Mr. Gunson?" "Well, what would happen, you know, if anything were to go wrong now?" "There's nothing could go wrong. We made sure of that when we built it didn't we?"

Mr. Craven tried to conceal from his superior the hint of exasperation which had crept into his voice but really, it was enough to try any man's patience. Caution was one thing but it was he, as the building contractor responsible for the supervision of the gangs of navvies, who had borne the brunt of their harsh tongues as the engineer had insisted that they toil in the mud to build a trench sixty feet deep across the valley rather than settle for the ten foot depth that the original plans specified for the bank's foundations. The rock had looked sound enough to him and even when the engineer's inspection satisfied them that a firm base had at last been reached the water had still been pouring in from those springs. That was more than two years ago. Since then his men had carted and dumped thousands and thousands of tons of sticky orange clay down that hole and then built up a watertight clay wall stretching right across the valley nearly a hundred feet high in the centre supported by sloping banks of graded stone and earth on either side. Mr. Craven could conceive of nothing which could endanger such a massive structure and would not himself have felt the matter urgent enough to demand such an arduous journey at this time of the night. He couldn't understand why Gunson hadn't sent a message to say that he would be there in the morning. But then he knew John Gunson.

The road now widened before plunging down the mean and narrow West Bar

Green and Gibraltar Street. The gaslamps flickered in the gusty wind and in their fitful pools of light groups of roughly-dressed working men and women, in thick trousers and caps or woollen shawls, emerged from dark alleys and narrow jennels, their wooden clogs clattering, to make their way towards one of the seven public houses whose windows lit this short stretch of road. Most of the women carried babies bundled in heavy shawls against the chill wind. As the gig passed by the open door of The Old Tankard Inn John Gunson's ears picked up the sounds of singing and raised voices, although they were still not attuned to the broad Irish accents. Many Irish people had recently settled in this poor part of town, seeking employment in the new steelworks or following work on the railways. Many had been driven from their own country by the horror of famine following the potato blight which had struck their crops. Although Gunson didn't approve of the drunkenness which prevailed in these poorer areas of the town he could well sympathise with people who were forced by circumstance to live and work in such squalid conditions.

Not for the first time John Gunson felt like an outsider in the town in which he had lived for most of his life. Sheffield was changing and growing so rapidly that he sometimes did not feel part of it. Many of the little workshops around here, which for a hundred years had rung to the sound of the knife forgers' hammers, now housed a far wider collection of tradesmen. Bootmakers, tailors, and joiners occupied many of the premises and only one in five betrayed their local origins by still speaking in the old 'Shevvild' dialect. He rarely ventured into the warren of unsavoury courtyards of 'back-to-back' dwellings consisting of poorly-built and insanitary two room cottages where working people attempted to raise their children, few of whom would live to adulthood.

He glanced to his left as they passed a once imposing house surrounded by iron railings at the bottom of Lambert Street. In a short stretch of five of the crowded courtyards on this narrow street, which led up the hill towards the debtors' gaol on Scotland Street, were a hundred and fifty inhabitants in twenty one meagre cottages, as well as the lean-to workshops of spring knife cutlers, scissor makers and a Britannia metal manufacturer, Mr William Howe. Such living conditions had already been condemned in the Sanitary Report, to which Mr. Gunson had given evidence in 1848. He had been appalled by the graphic accounts of filth, lack of sanitation and inadequate water supply which were portrayed. He could now understand why more than half of the infants born into such conditions did not survive their first birthday, and felt a responsibility on his own shoulders to play his part in bringing a fresh water supply to these families for washing, cleaning and drinking. Never again, he hoped, would the scourge of cholera visit these dark alleys as it had only thirty years before, though malaria and typhoid still took their toll.

To the right, as the gig passed the end of Bower Street, the forbidding mass of the Sheffield Union Workhouse was visible against the speeding clouds, representing that dreaded destiny of those of their fellow townspeople who could no longer support themselves. The road now widened out in Shalesmoor and the travellers could put such grim considerations behind them as the buildings took on a grander scale. To the right the tall chimney of Mr. James Dixon's Cornish Works, where such exquisite pieces of silverware and plate were produced in a thousand intricate designs to grace the tables of dukes, princes and Maharajahs, stood proud above the brick buildings. The imposing rear facade of Dixon's, with its dozens of rounded windows, rose directly from the river to the left of Ball Street Bridge. Looking to the right from the bridge the river divided, a channel cutting off a piece of land which had become known as Kelham Island, after Kelham Homer, the town armourer, who had his workshop here in the sixteenth century. The island still thundered to the rumblings of its steel rolling mills.

As the road forked into three, the gig followed the right hand fork along the much improved turnpike rather than the old Low Road which ran alongside the River Don. They passed the Don Brewery and John Gunson reflected, not for the first time, that Sheffield was a town of smells, and that the acrid odour of brewing hops from the steaming vats of the thirty local breweries which filled the night air was preferable to many others that the town had to offer. They sped past the comfortingly familiar dark shape of St. Philip's church, and Mr. Gunson, from long habit, pulled his watch from his waistcoat pocket, flicked open its face, and checked the time against the clock on the tower. Nine fifteen, and still only just leaving the town. He quickly reckoned that it would be ten before he reached Dale Dyke. At the earliest. He mentally urged the horse on, desperate to know what was happening at his dam. Behind the church the grandly classical facade of the Globe Cutlery and Steel Works stretched along the road, its dark shape outlined by the brilliant red glow front the crucible steel furnaces in the yard behind.

Sarah Jane Green lived with her uncle and aunt at Eagle Works across the river from Kelham Island. She finished her piano practice and knelt up at the window overlooking the river. She could just see the weir below Ball Street bridge. Even in the dark the water could clearly be seen as it turned a foaming white, roaring over the weir. Weeks of heavy rain had brought the River Don to its highest level for many years. Above even that noise Sarah could clearly hear the occasional shrieks of Mr. Eaton's pig from the cottages at the head of Kelham Island. Straight across the river the glow, the billowing smoke and the constant rumbling from Kelham Rolling Mills was difficult to ignore. Beyond these steel works stood the Union Workhouse. At times over a thousand Sheffield's poorest inhabitants, from babes in arms to the oldest, lived and had to work within its walls. A shiver went down her spine. She might well have been sent there had it not been for her aunt and uncle. However, as her aunt kept reminding her, she must write that letter to her grandmother in Leeds. That was a more pleasant thought.

As if it caught John Gunston's thoughts, the horse picked up speed as they passed the elegant tall railings and twin gatehouses which stood between the road and the three-storied General Infirmary. The buildings had thinned out and the lights of the town were left behind. Although one or two fields still separated this edge of the town from the cluster of houses and factories at Philadelphia, most of the open spaces were already being built on and a ragged ribbon of development stretched for the couple of miles to the village of Hillsborough. The road here ran along the lower slope of the hillside which runs up towards the old village of Crookes below which, on Crookes Moor, still stood the series of seven or eight small dams which until only thirty years before had adequately provided for the water needs of the town. Fresh thoughts broke through the regular rhythm of the horses hooves and the beating rain to trouble Mr. Gunson's mind and he only found reassurance for his concerns in thinking back over the part that he had played in the accomplishments of the Sheffield Waterworks Company since its incorporation in 1830. No one could possibly criticise the energy with which the company had embarked on new constructions. John Gunson had been involved in the building of the three Redmires reservoirs on the western moors and in the construction of the Rivelin reservoirs. Although there was much work still to do, his strong sense of service to the people of Sheffield gave Mr. Gunson a certain satisfaction, for now three times the number of houses could be provided with a water supply than in 1830 and he felt again the pang of excitement that the completion of the reservoirs of the 'Bradfield Scheme' of which the Dale Dyke was to be the first, was finally to bring a constant supply of fresh water to meet the needs of all the householders and industrialists in the town. Surely nothing could go wrong now, after these ten long years planning and building, to hold up the completion of the scheme still further.

His thoughts were interrupted by Mr. Craven. From this point there was a clear view across a field on the right to the River Don in the bottom of the valley. Although in the darkness the men could not pick out the black waters of the river itself, the contractor was pointing out to Mr. Gunson the long dirty white line which stretched diagonally across the river, indicating the position of the massive weir which directed the water along the goits to feed the wheels of yet another of the dozens of mills stretched along the river. It was the huge volume of water which was pounding over this weir which had caught the attention of Mr. Craven and the two men again remarked on the last month's exceptionally high rainfall which had swollen the usually lazy flowing river to a torrent. Here, at Neepsend, the goit or channels to the Philadelphia Steel Works actually cut off a bend in the river. To the people who lived in the dozen or so cottages on this piece of land, attached to the rest of Sheffield only by bridges over the stinking Don, it had long been known as Bacon Island. Some of them worked in the tilt forge and the rolling mill powered by the water where the steel, melted elsewhere, was heated to red heat and pounded or rolled into shape. The regular beating of the forge hammers seemed to shake the ground. As they looked across to the collection of dark cottages and terraced rows clustered just across the river along Neepsend Lane, the two men wondered how these people could live beside such a noisy neighbour. Gunson found himself imagining the scene with the additional seven hundred million gallons of water which a sudden collapse of his embankment would release to cascade down the valley, but quickly put such fanciful ideas aside as unthinkable.

Behind the houses a train steamed up the valley on the opposite side to the travellers, going north out of Sheffield on its way to Manchester through the Woodhead Tunnel. The railway line was set on an embankment, putting the train on a level with the gig, and for a little time the two kept pace until the train disappeared into the dark mass of Old Park Wood which stretched up the steep valley side. "It's an ill wind that blows nobody any good," thought Gunson now that they were beyond Neepsend and the pungent stink of the tanneries had been blown eastwards giving them hardly a whiff of the disgusting ingredients used in the process of tanning the leather. Not only were strong chemicals involved, which stained the river and killed all life in it, as well as large quantities of oak bark, but each of the three local tanneries here had their own recipes for what else went into the tanning pit. This included such unsavoury ingredients as large amounts of dogs' droppings and of urine.

The road now swung to the right around the austere stone walls of the old infantry barracks. Looking down the steep Wood Lane, the old wooden footbridge over the river, which linked the streets of cottages at Hillfoot with the acres of ground set out as pleasure gardens, small-holdings and allotments around Fairfield House on the other side, could be seen. Parts of this extensive area between the bend in the river and the railway embankment was laid out in formal patterns of trees and shrubs where the fashionable would promenade. One such was known as the Victoria Gardens. Smoke rose from the chimneys of the many small dwellings and buildings dotted over the rectangular plots. Some of the buildings simply stored the tools and materials of the gardeners but other one-storey cottages were occupied by poorer families who eked out a slender living from the produce of their garden and by keeping a few animals. Most had a pig and a few chickens and some kept rabbits.

The regular rhythmic trotting of the horses hooves now faded into the background of Mr. Gunson's busy mind as he mentally considered the different scenarios which could be conjured from the sketchy information that he had been given. George Swinden was at the scene. A trustworthy and efficient man, Mr. Swinden. One of the contractors. Hopefully he would already be opening the valves to release water through the twin eighteen inch diameter pipes which passed through the embankment. That would begin to release the pressure on the top part of the wall to some extent but it would be too slow to make an appreciable effect. He again went through the calculations which were the basis for the specifications of the dam wall drawn up by Mr. Leather, the consulting engineer. The 700 million gallons of water would be producing a force of 3 million tons on the embankment. The pipes would release 10,000 cubic feet per minute so it would take some 190 hours to empty the reservoir should this ever be necessary.

"I must get in touch with Mr. Leather as soon as possible," thought Gunson, "He won't be pleased. There has been more than enough delay already. He'll think back to the problems that we had with the embankment at Redmires, when it was damaged by repeated slips in 1848. There was no problem there in the end though. This will most probably be the same."

John Towlerton Leather, a member of a well known Yorkshire family of engineers, lived in some style in a grand house at Leventhorpe on the outskirts of Leeds. Until 1846 he was the resident engineer and surveyor to the waterworks company but now, as the consulting engineer, he was responsible for drawing up the plans and specifications which were then acted upon by John Gunson. It was some time since he had actually visited the Loxley Valley. Indeed, had the contractors not encountered so many problems in finding an impervious base for the puddle trench he would probably have visited even less than the once or twice a year that the situation had demanded. As it was, Mr. Leather's Friday evening could carry on uninterrupted by the events which were now unfolding far from his home, but which would so fearfully alter the course of the rest of his life.

* * * * * * * * * * * *

At the Dale Dyke embankment the contractors were justifying the faith placed in them by Mr. Gunson by taking any measures which they could to put to rest the fears of those neighbours who now anxiously clustered around the crack on the bank, clutching cloaks or shawls tightly around themselves against the biting wind. Only their faces were visible, lit by the guttering lanterns which one by one were blowing out. These locals had long lived beside the massive building works and had mixed feelings regarding the dam's construction in their quiet valley. Some entirely resented the monstrous intrusion which the great wall and its army of navvies represented, challenging and changing their age old way of life. Others, however, looked to the previously unknown prosperity which the valley was enjoying. As well as those employed directly on the construction teams, local tradesmen were kept busy supplying the contractors needs and the majority of the hundreds of labourers, who had been recruited from elsewhere, had relatively comfortable lodgings with local families. A few of the older workers remembered the appalling hardships that they had endured during the winters when digging the Woodhead railway tunnel across the bleak moorland only a few miles to the north in the early 1840s.

Opinions were expressed by those present regarding the cause of the crack and the possible danger that it might represent. "This is just a crack caused by the settlement of the inner part of the embankment," said Mr. Swinden, one of the contractors present. "I agree. The water has penetrated the top of the embankment, making it lean over a little towards the water," added Mr. Fountain, the other contractor. "Then you say there's no danger?" asked Mr. Ibbotson, who as usual stepped forward to speak on behalf of the concerned villagers of Bradfield. "None whatsoever. This is all quite usual," replied the contractors, not even giving serious consideration to the unthinkable alternative.

One by one the villagers, not without misgivings, accepted the glib reassurances, and with many murmurings and much shaking of heads made their way back down the embankment and set off in groups back to their own cottages and farmsteads down the valley. Keeping company with Joseph Ibbotson, the miller from Low Bradfield, was a group consisting of Joseph Dawson, the village tailor, and Mr. Nicholls, the schoolmaster, as well as Joseph Ibbotson's brothers, William and Richard. The Ibbotsons had been regular visitors to the site and had frequently been employed on the construction from the first. It was therefore not surprising that their views on the significance of this ominous crack were now eagerly sought by their companions. "I know that they say it's all safe," said Mr. Nicholls, "but I find it difficult to have complete faith in a bank that's built of nothing but earth and clay when I see all that water built up behind it." "It's not the bank itself that worries me," replied the miller, "I still worry about what lies beneath it!" "Aye," continued Richard, "You remember when we were at the bottom of that great trench the day they started filling it with puddled clay? They were still having to pump the water out from those springs." "Yes, but that's not what I meant though. I still say that the rock hereabouts is not strong enough to support all that weight safely."

'The scene was one of painful interest and excitement.'

Certainly, following test drillings early on, it had been decided that the whole embankment should be constructed a hundred and fifty yards upstream from the line originally proposed, as far away as was possible without incurring the inconvenient delay of the passing of a new Act of Parliament. This was due to the discovery that the exact spot had been subject to a series of landslips and disturbances which ran diagonally across the valley towards the Walkers' farm on the north side. The agitated speculations continued as the men paced briskly along the dark road. Joseph voiced his added misgivings regarding the construction of the dam wall. "I still don't think they ever gave the layers chance to settle properly before the next layer was tipped on. I think that's what's happening now. Stands to reason. The whole thing's bound to settle for a long time to come."

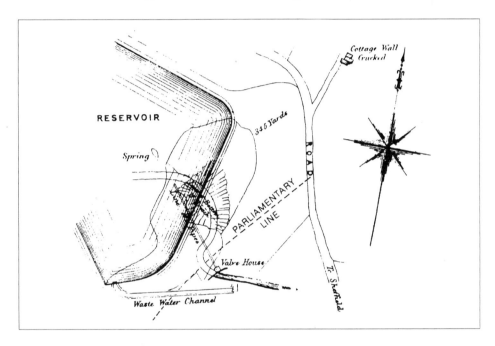

But to William the strange coincidence of his wife's unsettling dream of the previous night and the fissure in the embankment had been more than chance could explain. He repeated the dream to his attentive audience, even though they had all heard the story earlier in the day. "She woke up in a real fright, I can tell you. I've never known her do it before neither. "Oh William," she says to me, "I thought I were drowned, I did. I were trying to get across this narrow bridge and there were water all round me. I couldn't get across and I couldn't get back. I thought I were done for, but just as the water was washing me away I woke up." Now I can't believe that it's right for a new embankment to crack like that. Even if it turns out that there is no danger I'm not for my bed tonight. I'm keeping me clothes on, ready for off!" "Aye, I think I'll be happier if I know t'children are safe," said his brother Richard. "Is it all right if I bring them up to spend the night with you Joseph? The water won't reach up to your cottage even if the dam were to burst." "Of course you can. Bring them all round directly, if you're sure it's worth getting the poor little mites out of their beds on a night like this."

By this time the group had reached the little village and were crossing the stone bridge over the Loxley, which tumbled tunefully over rocks between steep ferny banks. They passed the Wesleyan Chapel and came to the smart new school adjoining the schoolhouse with its pretty garden down to the river. Mr. Nicholls bid his companions goodnight and hurried into the house to reassure his anxious wife and to go to bed. But Jane, his wife, was not content to rest. Together they went out again and, as they stood on the school bridge watching the stream flow below them, there came a sudden surge of water, filling the bed of the river. Jane was further alarmed. "What's happening?" she exclaimed. "Is this the start of a flood?" "No Jane, They will be releasing some of the water to ease the pressure on the dam, that's all. It will all be safe now. Lets go in to bed." "You go up if you wish," she replied as they re-entered the house, "I couldn't sleep yet." and she threw a shovelful of coal on the fire. "I'll just sit here, by the fire, until this has burned down."

Joseph Dawson and his brother were the next to take their leave, as they now hurried into their cottage, the lowest in a row stretching towards the river bank. Joseph was particularly anxious to get back home and see that all was well with his wife whom he had left in bed with their new baby boy, born only the day before. As he hurried into the small front bedroom he smiled to see his wife sitting up in the bed, cradling their new baby in her arms. This was their second son, their four year old was sleeping in the back room with his uncle. Joseph undressed and settled himself into bed beside his wife and baby.

The Ibbotsons reached their own cottage doors. Joseph was last since his house stood above the others overlooking his mill. Neither William nor Richard had any intention of settling down to their beds. Richard wasted no time in rousing his five children, who, with much complaining and rubbing of eyes, were shepherded up the hill to their uncle's house where they were made as comfortable as possible. William sat by his fireside smoking his pipe, fully dressed 'so as to be ready for off'.

Meanwhile, back at Dale Dyke, the contractors had sent four or five workmen to the valvehouse at the foot of the embankment to open the valves which would release water through the twin outlet pipes while they went to the far side to see if the water level had yet reached the level of the overflow weir. Despite the strength of the wind, against which they struggled, the contractors made their way along the embankment top, not yet apprehending any danger. The valves were jammed, probably because of the great pressure of water on them. Opening them took at least half an hour of heaving and levering, but at last they were released, letting the water roar out, the vibrations shaking the ground on which the men stood. The water level in the reservoir was now only a few inches below the overflow but, confident that all had been done to ensure the safety of the dam, Mr. Swinden and Mr. Fountain instructed the men to shelter and waited to see if Mr. Gunson would arrive with fresh instructions.

* * * * * * * * * * *

Mr. Gunson's gig was now running down towards Hillsborough Bridge, passing the extremely imposing mass of the new barracks on his right. The toll keeper looked out and, recognising him, waved his curious acknowledgment to the engineer. Here the road crossed the Loxley and, following this valley, the engineer's gig turned left up Holme Lane. Beside the bridge white water foamed over another massive stone built weir which diverted a supply of water into the dam of Mr. Hawksley's mill at Owlerton. The travellers were quiet, tired after an already full day's work, but Mr. Gunson's thoughts still raced. They passed Brick Row on their right, an ugly and poorly built terrace of three story dwellings, and approached Malin Bridge, where the lighted windows and sounds of good-hearted merriment from The Stag Inn seemed to invite them in from the cold. The little village was itself little more than a cluster of cottages and a couple of pubs and farms centered on the old corn mill by the bridge, where the Rivelin joins the Loxley. Here the road forks to the left up the hill to Stannington or straight up the valley to Loxley. It was a lively community of a couple of hundred people, many employed in or connected with the local trades.

"How I wish we were enjoying Mrs. Armitage's hospitality at The Stag tonight, Mr. Gunson. She brews some of the finest beer for miles." "Maybe, but we may well have a long night ahead of us yet, and we will certainly need a clear head" replied the engineer, quite astonished that such an idea could even enter his companion's head at a time like this. On other, more auspicious occasions, Mr. Craven, as well as many of the workers on the dam, had frequently enjoyed the convivial company of this particular hostelry, although the rival establishment on the other side of the road, The Malin Bridge Inn, for some unknown reason better known to the locals as 'The Cleakum Inn', could also claim a loyal band of regulars. There was nobody hereabouts who did not know the landlady of The Stag, Mrs. Elizabeth Armitage, although it was her son and his wife, William and Anne who now did most of the heavy work as well as help to see to the needs of the two lodgers, Henry Hall and James Frith, and bring up the five children including baby Maria. Elizabeth Crownshaw, the new servant girl, was proving her worth with the customers in the evening and, when there were heavy barrels to move, William could always count on his brother Greaves, who lived next door, to lend a hand. Not only were the family well known publicans, however, they had long been the managers and, since 1842 the owners, of Mousehole Forge, a few hundred yards up the Rivelin Valley. Both Greaves and William worked with their father and brothers at the forge, and many a blacksmith's hammer rang true as it struck an anvil with the distinctive Mousehole mark.

MOUSEHOLE FORGE

21

'Proceeding down the valley, we come now and then upon grinding wheels, worked by water power, which were erected and in operation long before the application of steam to the general purposes of industry.'

Other than the Armitages, the family with which most locals were most likely to have been acquainted, were the Trickets, whose substantial farmhouse and outbuildings the travellers could now see behind the corn mill on the opposite side of the river. Its extensive gardens and orchards sloping down to the water's edge. The farm was successful and the family were one of the most prosperous in the locality, but this had not prevented them from being as familiar as most of their less well-off neighbours with that heartbreak that comes from the early loss of their children. For Elizabeth to have suffered the death of five children in infancy seemed, to all who knew the couple, to have been particularly cruel. They had buried Mary Ann, aged 4 months, in 1845, Elizabeth, 13 months, in 1848, Maria, 8 months, in 1854, Sophia, aged 9 months, in 1858, and the latest baby had been laid to rest with her sisters in the windswept graveyard at High Bradfield only two months before. Such tragic losses seemed to have bound the remaining members of the family closely together, for 12 year old Jemima, 11 year old James and George, still only five, were unusually dutiful and loving children. Tonight the house was yet again in mourning. On Wednesday they had attended the funeral of Mrs. Tricket's mother and had persuaded her father that he should come and stay with them for a while. Today they had spent a busy day helping him to move a few of his personal possessions into his new home although, as he had been constantly reminding them, he was not embarking on this without misgivings about leaving his own house at View Fold, over the hill.

Despite the extensive size of the Tricket's farmhouse the coming of Thomas Kay, Elizabeth's father, to stay entailed some domestic reorganisation. The three servants would still need their lodgings but, regrettably, it would no longer be possible to accommodate Joseph Barker, the young man who was in partnership with Mr. Johnson at the nearby Limerick Wheel, where they were having great success making the wire for the new crinoline dresses. This was his last night at the farmhouse. He was moving back to his former lodgings at Mrs. Bower's tomorrow, after he had paid the men their wages which he had collected from Sheffield earlier, and which he was now checking before settling down for the night.

The road now swung sharply to the left, closely following the Loxley. Beyond Malin Bridge, although the road was straight and wide, the horse struggled against both the weather and the gradient. Comforting settlements were behind them and there were still four or five miles to go; they were less than half way to the dam. Although the road itself became increasingly bleak, the travellers could look to their left into the valley bottom and be reassured that human activity continued despite the ferocious weather. For the next miles, until they reached Bradfield the presence of a whole series of twelve mills beading the river was indicated by glowing furnace chimneys, the dim moonlight occasionally reflecting on a mill dam and the pounding of hammers. The road passed quite close to the two dams and mills of Wisewood Forge and Rolling Mil,l where the rumble of machinery and the glinting water splashing over the revolving wheel was all that betrayed the busy scenes of industry inside, where scythes were being forged and steel rolled into red hot snaking lengths by men constantly wiping the sweat from their brow despite the winter cold outside. Accidents were common enough in these forges but it was the dust thrown off the grindstones in the valley's many grinding hulls which was the real killer, being made up of a deadly cocktail of silica and steel particles. Few grinders lived to see forty.

John Gunson cast a more than casual eye over the extensive area of mill buildings. The works were well known to him, as were the proprietors of the many mills, for he had been involved in the long and acrimonious negotiations between the Water Company and the mill owners over the rights to a guarantee of compensation water so that the wheels would keep turning despite the impounding of the upper valley to collect drinking water. Mr. Horn at Wisewood, the Chapmans at Little Matlock and Mr. Woodward, the paper maker, at Olive Wheels, all were familiar names as the gig trotted on past successive mills. In the event the industrialists, backed by the land owners, had demonstrated their power dramatically, for the agreement with the Company assured them of water to power the mills year round, six days a week, a level of supply which they had never enjoyed before. The Dale Dyke dam was being built to ensure this supply of compensation water, although its pent up water was to descend on the valley's mills far sooner than anyone could know, and with devastating results.

Only one light shone out on the opposite valley side, and its appearance immediately recalled happy times spent with his family and friends for Mr. Gunson. The light shone from The Rock Inn, standing above the steep wooded slopes of this, the most dramatically picturesque, section of the valley. Small sandstone cliffs outcrop here and, between these, paths and walkways had been laid out for the enjoyment of weekend and summer evening promenaders. The inn had been built especially to take advantage of the attractions of the scenery and the area had been dubbed 'Little Matlock', although the scenery couldn't really compare to the Derbyshire resort. Still, there were visitors enough from Sheffield to be entertained by the landlord's retellings of the old local legend of the area's association with Robin Hood, or 'Robin of Loxley'. The engineer smiled to himself, remembering days in the previous summer when he and Charlotte had been all too ready for refreshment after climbing the steep path back up to the inn.

It was not until the gig came towards the little village of Damflask that Mr. Gunson's thoughts became sharply focussed again. The men were at first slightly bewildered by an unfamiliar scene of busy activity. From the farmhouse to the left a whole family, it appeared, were busily occupied by the light of lanterns taking furniture and belongings from the house and piling them onto a cart. A young man was noisily herding cows from the barn towards a field on the other side of the road. All was hurry and bustle.

The engineer's blood ran cold on realising that these frantic preparations were in response to young Stephenson's warning. All along the road the scene was repeated, the sparse population doing what it could to protect itself and its belongings by moving to higher ground. Here the road swung close to the river, which it crossed at this point by an old stone bridge. This road swept up the hill to the south towards the villages of Stannington and Dungworth, whilst the road up the Loxley Valley carried on towards Bradfield. This crossroads was the focus of the little settlement of Damflask. Beside the bridge stood The Barrel Inn and a small group of cottages, whilst the village corn mill stood a little further above the bridge. The miller, Joseph Hobson, lived in a cottage on the opposite side of the road to his mill. As John Gunson's carriage swung round beside The Barrel Inn he became even more disturbed by the busy and alarming preparations which were underway.

* * * * * * * * * * *

The innkeeper, Joseph Ibbotson, on receiving the frightening news from Stephenson Fountain earlier that evening, had clearly wasted no time in passing it on to the other villagers, who in their turn, passed it on themselves. It could be counted on that the dire warnings would have lost none of their menace in the retelling. Now, hearing the thud of horses hooves and seeing the familiar figure of the chief engineer hurrying up towards Dale Dyke so late at night, all heads turned and few now had any doubts about the gravity of their situation. At the first of the cottages behind the Barrel Inn, Mr. Joseph Walton had drawn up a horse and a cart to transport his wife and new baby, only two days old, to safety. Outside the open door of the cottage an agitated argument was taking place between Walton and his neighbours, Thomas Kirk and Henry Horsfield, as he attempted to coax his reluctant wife out of the house. " Thy'll kill her if thy tries to take her away on this, Joseph, when she's only just had the child, Don't be so foolish. Let her be." "Aye, Henry's right Joseph," replied Thomas Kirk. "After all we don't know that there will be a flood. Harry, as lodges with me, reckons there's nowt to fret over, and he should know, he works on t'dam." " Oh leave me Joseph, leave me," pleaded Mrs. Walton from her bed, "Let's bide here. You might as well let me go down in flood as catch my death of cold on this wagon." But Joseph was determined. The neighbours eventually helped him to place the bed on the cart and carry his wife and children to safety on it. Thomas Kirk still considered this a foolish act and his lodger, 'Sheffield Harry' as he was called by the villagers, thought the whole thing a great joke. The two were still laughing as they entered the cottage and closed the door on the cold night wind.

Only a short time later, however, they were roused by a knocking on the door. Thomas Kirk again opened the door. Outside, in the driving rain, stood Mr. Shaw, the proprietor of Damflask wire mill, which stood a little way below the bridge. He stepped into the light and pulled off his wet top hat. "Good Evening Mr. Kirk, I'm sorry to call on you at such an hour but I've heard rumours of a crack in the embankment up at Dale Dyke. I was wondering if your lodger thought there was any real cause for alarm." "No, he was up there himself this afternoon, Mr. Shaw, and he reckons there's nothing in it at all." "No, don't you worry Mr. Shaw" said Harry, stepping up to them, "there's nowt will shift that lot I can tell you. In fact I'm off to bed missen now, so I wish you goodnight." "Goodnight Harry, and goodnight to you, Mr. Kirk. I had intended to go down to the mill to warn the four lads that are working tonight but I see that I've no cause to alarm them after all. Goodnight."

The miller, meanwhile, was acting with all haste to protect his belongings from the impending flood. After all, Joseph Hobson had everything to lose. Both his mill and his cottage were close to the river, and in them was everything that he owned. He looked out from the door of the mill to see the carriage hurry past and quickly set to work with renewed vigour to draw up sack after heavy sack on the rope hoist and carefully stack it on the upper floor of the mill, where it would be safely stored above the level of any rising water. Satisfied only when all was secure, he went home and took his wife to a cottage a little way up the valley and returned to drive his two cows and his horse to a higher field.

* * * * * * * * * * * *

Had there been any remaining doubt in Mr. Gunson's mind regarding the necessity of his present journey it was now entirely dispelled. His apprehension was almost unbearable. The dark road seemed endless and he felt completely powerless, realising that the fate of so many lives could well depend on his actions. The terrifying consequences of the bursting of a dam of this size were well known to him, and he knew that it could happen. He shuddered as he recalled hearing the terrible news of the collapse of the Bilberry Dam at Holmfirth only ten miles to the north, almost exactly twelve years before. As well as causing terrible destruction, the midnight flood had killed 95 people. But, if he was honest, John Gunson recalled with clearest horror the terrible condemnation of the chief engineer, Mr. Leather's uncle, George Leather, and the overseers of the construction by the inquest jury, who would have brought a charge of manslaughter against them if they had not constituted a corporation and thus been exempt from personal blame. But to be found guilty of neglect and mismanagement would be devastating enough. "No, there has been no neglect at Dale Dyke, and certainly no mismanagement. Such an accident could surely never be repeated!" But the possibility remained, however much he tried to put it from his mind.

The valley deepened beyond Damflask, the enclosing rim of hills now being capped in bleak moorland. Lower down, the steep valley sides were divided into a pattern of rectangular fields surrounded by neat sandstone walls. Here and there prosperous-looking farm buildings were dotted across the landscape, huddling from the prevailing wind behind groups of tall trees. Now that he could see the lights of the village of High Bradfield twinkling high on the valley side to the right, Mr. Gunson knew that there was not far to go. He expected the people of Low Bradfield to be in a similar state of agitated activity as he had witnessed at Damflask but, as the gig passed the first few cottages and came to Mr. Ibbotson's corn mill beside the river, it was somewhat reassuring to see that all was relatively quiet. "It looks as if the panic is all over", said Mr. Craven. "If there had still been any danger these people would know about it. After all, many of the labourers lodge in the village." "Let's hope so", replied Mr. Gunson. By way of further reassurance a friendly voice shouted a greeting. As they drew alongside the men recognised one of the labourers. "Ah, Mr. Gunson, Mr. Craven, evenin' to you sirs". "Good evening Sam. Can you tell us how things are?" "Aye, it's a shame they got you out. It were nowt to worry about after all." "You mean everything's safe?" "Aye, right as rain. But there's Mr. Swinden still up there, he'll tell you. I'm off home to get missen warm an' dry. Goodnight." "Goodnight Sam."

'Mr. Gunson and Mr. Craven, with all speed, hasten to the spot where the crack has been discovered. Mr. Fountain says if we don't relieve the dam of water, there'll be a blow-up in half an hour.'

Samuel Harrison

The Stricken Dam

In a little less than a mile the great dark mass of the embankment reared up across the valley. Mr. Gunson again drew out his pocket watch. By the dim light he could just make out that it was shortly after ten o'clock. As they came nearer, lights could be seen moving across the slope, groups of workmen inspecting its muddy surface. The horse, steaming in the cold air and hot breath snorting from its nostrils, was brought to a relieved standstill. A workman with a lantern hurried up to help the impatient engineer from the carriage. Mr. Gunson wasted no time making his way up the embankment for he could see the site contractors at the top. As he reached the group of men, the wind, blasting the slanting rain down the valley, cut through his heavy clothes and he pulled his hat down and drew his cloak tightly around him. "Where is this crack then, Swinden?" asked Gunson, immediately assuming control but feeling increasingly doubtful that it had been really necessary for him to be here. "It's over there Mr. Gunson," replied Swinden, pointing towards the centre of the embankment. "They've opened the pipes fully."

A couple of workmen led the men to the place. About twelve feet from the top a narrow gash could be seen running some fifty yards along. "Give me more light." Gunson crouched to closely examine the crack. It was just wide enough to push his hand in and seemed to extend straight down. The engineer spent a few moments pondering the significance of this. The crack was not wide but he was under no illusions that in this position in the centre of the dam wall any weakness was potentially dangerous. He turned and climbed back to the summit from which he looked out over the rough expanse of water. The wind raised it into little peaks and whisked an uncomfortable spray into the men's faces. Whatever his feelings about the potential danger of the crack Mr. Gunson clearly had no concern for the embankment's immediate stability. Otherwise he would not have now been standing directly above the crack. Otherwise he would have dispatched messengers with all haste to warn the sleepers in the valley below.

The level of the water in the reservoir was almost certainly higher than it had been earlier in the day despite the pipes having been opened. Mr. Gunson now led the group across the dam wall to the far side in order to see if the water was escaping over the masonry wall and down the stepped slope of the waste weir. To his dismay he saw that it was still a few inches from the top and was not yet running over, indicating to him that the reservoir had yet further to fill. Mr. Fountain voiced everyone's fears. "If we don't relieve the pressure of water against the embankment I fear that we'll lose it within half an hour, Mr. Gunson," he shouted against the wind. "I fear you could be right. The dam is still filling. If we lower the masonry of the weir here we could at least prevent it from filling any further."

While Fountain was instructing the men to fetch gunpowder to blow a hole in the top of the weir Mr. Gunson hurried down to the valve house at the foot of the bank to check how much water was being released. He and Swinden checked and rechecked the dials with intense frustration that they could not lower the water more quickly, even though they both knew that to do so would be extremely dangerous in itself for, if the vast weight of water pushing against the dam wall was to be released too quickly, the whole of the inside of the embankment could slump. They then climbed back up the embankment to take another look at the crack.

The workmen by this time had, with enormous difficulty because of the wind and rain, succeeded in laying gunpowder into a hole in the closely fitting stone blocks. The fuse was laid and the men crouched to shelter from the blast as it was lit. Nothing happened. They tried again. Again nothing. Maybe the powder was wet or could it be that they have laid it too hurriedly? On reporting their failure to Mr. Gunson, he ordered them to get back and try again, his anxiety and tiredness now beginning to show.

He and Swinden returned to examine the crack once more, Gunson still unsure about its cause. He wondered if the cracking extended into the puddle clay core, so the two men set about measuring the distance to the top of the wall to establish if the water in the dam was at the same level. Intent on making careful measurements Mr. Gunson was stooping over his lantern at one end of the crack. On glancing up again he couldn't quite believe his eyes. A foaming white sheet of water was flowing over the embankment. It rushed towards him and plunged down the widening gap. Thinking quickly he shouted to George Swinden. "I'm going to the valve house to see how much water we're losing." He made his way, more cautiously now, down the embankment and into the small building. The others were following down the slope but realised that they were no longer safe. Swinden shouted a warning to Mr. Gunson to come out and, as the engineer emerged he looked up, his whole life of fifty five years seeming to have led up to this moment. As if in slow motion a central segment of the top of the wall, about thirty feet wide, was collapsing and with a great rumble a white torrent taking its place. Gunson stood transfixed. Swinden was fortunately close enough to grab his arm and pull him out of the path of the surging water and, as they fled across the base of the embankment, the ground shuddered and the whole central portion was swept away.

As they ran another loud explosion above them revealed that the gunpowder had ignited, blowing a now pointless hole in the waste weir. The volume of water crashing through the breach in the dam was awesome. It was as if the great basin of high Pennine moorland was tilting, tipping its contents down into that narrow wooded channel. To most people the power demonstrated when colossal natural forces are unleashed is quite incomprehensible. We can only marvel at those pictures of wheat straws which have been forced through solid wooden gateposts by the power within a freak American tornado and we can't quite come to terms with the fact that such a normally yielding medium as water can be so transformed in nature as to be capable of delivering blows as powerful as a massive steam hammer. But John Gunson, as he stood now gazing on the widening breach in impotent horror, was only too aware of the menace that now roared down the valley. He felt the blood draining from his face and released a gasp, experiencing a sickening churning in the pit of his stomach. It was as though he has been kicked hard beneath the ribs. "It's all up! The embankment is going," was all that his dry lips could utter. But quickly the adrenaline began to surge through his veins and take control. There was clearly no more that he could do here. His duty must be to

'It's all up. The embankment's going!'

George Swinden

31

warn as many people as possible who stood in the path of the flood. With a shout to Swinden he leaped into his carriage and the tired horse, spooked by the deafening roar of the water, was whipped into frenzied flight down the dark road. The engineer, having lost all track of the passage of time, pulled the heavy watch by its chain from his waistcoat pocket. Flicking open its face he was surprised to make out in the dim light that it was exactly midnight.

The horse quickly covered the three quarters of a mile between the dam and the first habitation, the farmstead of John Empsall and his family, which stood beside Annett bridge over the usually idyllic Loxley. The wild roar of the water still accompanied the engineer and he was horrified to see, as he jumped from the carriage and ran down the farm track, that even here he was too late. He found breath to shout a feeble warning but his words were drowned by the booming water.

As he stood watching, the wall of water hit the stone built house like a battering ram and swept it, together with the barns and outhouses, clean away. As he watched the roaring waves were already foaming over the spot. It was with tremendous relief, then, that John Gunson saw huddled figures hurrying towards him round the bend in the track, all still pulling clothes around themselves. Gunson recognised William Rose, one of the construction workers who lodged with the Empsalls. "Is everyone safe, Rose?" demanded Gunson. "Yes, we all got out, but it was a close thing. If it hadn't been for Thomas Fish running down to warn us about ten minutes ago we'd have had no chance. Did you see how the house went? I wouldn't have believed it. God help all them down the valley, that's all I can say." The terrified, homeless family, including the three children, now stood shaking and crying in the cold night wind. All that they possessed they now stood up in, and that was precious little. Even their obstinate pig and donkey had refused to be forced from their snug shelters, which were now no more. "God help them," repeated Gunson, shaking his head, "God help us all!"

Indeed, the fate of hundreds of unsuspecting innocent people now rested in the hands of the Almighty. The shattering wall of water was already far down the valley and even the fastest horse could not have overtaken it to convey a warning to them. Dale Dyke's chief engineer realised that he could have no further part in the night's grim proceedings.

Death and Destruction Down the Loxley

It was the eerie howling of the village dogs, their sharp ears being the first to catch the ominous rumblings from further up the valley, which alerted the villagers of Low Bradfield to the impending disaster from which the small settlement was never quite to recover. Next came men, running, shouting warnings and hammering on doors. "It's coming! Look out! Run for your lives! The dam's burst!" Those not already alerted now drowsily went to look out of the window to find out whose drunken carousing was disturbing their sleep. But by now the growing volume of noise, an indescribable noise, a hissing rumble, a thunderous roaring, vibrating through the air, could leave no one in any doubt of the danger they were in.

William Ibbotson at least was prepared. Rushing from his house he heard the shouted warnings and set about rousing his sleeping neighbours, amongst whom were the school master and his wife, Mr. and Mrs. Nicholls. "Escape for your lives! The flood's coming!" The Nicholls were quickly out of the house, across the road and onto the flight of stone steps leading into the sloping field opposite their house. Reaching the top of the steps, Jane turned and let out a scream of warning, seeing her foolish husband running back into the house. She could now see the pounding wall of water, three storeys high, bearing down on it. Her husband reappeared, pulling his arms into the overcoat which he had returned to fetch, and he only just reached the steps before the flood was level with the couple. They turned to watch as, before their unbelieving eyes, their house and the school crashed into the surging waves and were carried away. Windblown spray from the impact soaked them through.

They were not the only witnesses to the deluge. It now seemed that the whole village had been roused and stood in stunned huddles, most in their flimsy night clothes, shouting or screaming warnings, which could not carry above the roar of the flood, to the occupants of the cottages and houses which were still in its path. Amongst the onlookers stood Joseph Ibbotson, powerless to do anything but watch as the water smashed into his three storey mill. For a moment the sturdy building stood firm, with only its roof visible above the foaming waves, but then it subsided and was entirely carried away.

In the lowest of the cottages opposite the mill the Dawsons had, only a little time before, settled the new baby into his snug wooden box which served as a cradle beside their bed and settled themselves when they, too, were woken by the shouts. Joseph was in no doubt as to the cause of the noise. Quickly he directed his brother to take their four year old lad out to safety while he was left to consider how best to get his incapacitated wife and baby out. He ran into the street, reassuring her that he wouldn't leave her, to ask a passerby for help. But the man was intent on saving his own life, and hurried on. The alarming noise was getting louder as the tailor raced back up the stairs. His wife was now sitting on the edge of the bed cradling the baby, wrapped in a blanket. Half carrying them Joseph helped his wife down the stairs and out of the door. His heart pounding with exertion and fear, he now looked up to see, to his horror, that the water was bearing down on them. It was clear that they were not going to make it across to Richard Ibbotson's house before it hit them. "Turn back! Turn back!" screamed his wife in terror, but the water swooped around the couple and knocked Joseph off his feet. To recover himself he was forced to release hold of his wife. She staggered and the baby was washed from her arms, leaving her clutching the empty blanket. It was all that they could do to struggle through the deepening water to their stairs. Joseph pushed his sobbing wife up the stairs and they scarcely reached the top as the water crashed through both the front and back of the house, flooding it to a depth of six feet. Their position was still precarious and they shouted for help from the bedroom window to their neighbours and brother who stood below, anxiously awaiting news of their fate. Richard and Joseph Ibbotson, having seen what had happened to the mill, urged them to throw something across to form a bridge between the window and the steeply rising bank behind the house. With much effort the frightened couple managed to manoeuver the mattress through the window but it was too short to reach across to the bank and it fell into the swirling water. Richard, however, now hurried up with a ladder which served its purpose well. Mrs. Dawson was helped and coaxed across this makeshift bridge to safety and was taken to Joseph Ibbotson's where she was clothed and put to bed, sobbing and grieving with the cold, fright and shock at the appalling fate of her newborn son, only one day old.

There were many to comfort and tend to her, since thirty people from six families now crowded into the miller's house for shelter. Against many entreaties the tailor, still in his soaking night clothes, rushed out of the house again with his brother to the edge of the still foaming torrent, which swirled around his own house. Frantically the two men scanned the dark water for signs of the lost child, but it soon became apparent to the other villagers that there could be little hope of the poor baby surviving. "What's that? Look, there! " screamed Joseph, as a fragment of material momentarily broke the surface. His brother shook his head sadly. Amongst the flotsam of broken furniture, sacks, belongings washed from houses and the smashed trees and branches that swirled in the eddies it was impossible to be sure of anything."Come along, Joseph. It's no good. You'll catch your death." Stunned and shaking, the tailor at last allowed himself to be led back to the miller's crowded house to comfort his grieving wife.

The water swept on, spending none of its energy as might be expected, but rather gaining in power as if funnelled down the narrow valley. Just below Bradfield, George Hobson only just managed to get his infirm father up the stairs of their cottage before the water filled the ground floor, in which he slept. Next door George Wilson, hearing the noise whilst drinking at the nearby Plough Inn, rushed home to find his house partly destroyed, and a little way away Martin Hawke and his family, having been warned of the danger by their four lodgers who worked on the dam's construction, watched in horrified disbelief from a safe distance on the hillside above as their farmhouse, barns, stables and animals were completely swept away by the howling torrent. The brown flood roared down the valley, gouging great holes in the river banks as boulders swirled round like ten ton marbles, and tearing up trees which had withstood many winters' storms.

About a mile below Bradfield stood Roebuck House, an extensive farmstead, and cottages surrounded by trees at the foot of a slope running down to the river. In the two cottages nearest to the river lived William Marsden with his young wife, Selina, their child and four lodgers. Being well off the road the warning which had earlier been relayed down the valley had passed this group by, and so they had no knowledge at all of the peril their lives were in. As the flood bore down towards them William Marsden was the first to be roused by a noise which he could not identify. He got up to gaze out of the window into the darkness but could see nothing and his young wife told him to get back into bed. At this moment the house was shaken by a great crash as the water hit it and burst through the doors, filling the lower rooms and smashing their furniture against the ceiling.

'Mr. Marsden, with great presence of mind, broke a leg off the dressing table and, with this improvised instrument, knocked a hole through the ceiling of the bedroom.'

Samuel Harrison

"We're done!" shouted William, still not quite understanding what was happening but frightened beyond anything he could have imagined, and he grabbed the baby and hugged it, and his wife, close to him. "Now we shall at least be all found dead

Above: 'Mrs.Kirk returned across the bridge with the cat under one arm and the dog under the other.'   Samuel Harrison

Below: 'My wife was still undressed but I put her out of the window and she was carried across and taken to Mr. Joseph Ibbotson's'   Joseph Dawson

together," he shouted over the din. They watched in frozen horror as the water bubbled and swirled up the stairs towards them. The cottage, however, held firm against the battering and to their enormous relief they saw the level of the water stop rising as it reached the top step. They hugged each other tightly in the realisation that they may yet survive, although the danger still wasn't over by any means. William looked around. The only way to safety was up, through the ceiling. Quickly he tore a leg off the wooden dressing table and then, standing on the bed, he set about hacking an untidy hole, through which he could see the night sky. He pulled himself through and was soon sitting outside on the wet, stone flagged roof. He could now see that he had not been alone in attempting this escape route. On the adjoining roof the Tittcombe family and their lodgers were emerging one by one from a similar opening a few feet away and then jumping from the edge of the roof onto the hillside beyond the swirling water. William leaned down into the hole and Selina handed him the baby, which he grasped under one arm whilst pulling his wife up with the other. A frightening leap into the darkness now landed him safely onto the higher ground at the back of the cottage. He stood and shouted to his wife who threw him the baby before jumping herself.

The forlorn group now stood safe but shivering in the field. They all made their way up the hill to the nearby Rock Farm, where a chilly welcome awaited them. Thinking that they were a group of burglars, the recently widowed mistress of the house refused to open the door to them until she eventually recognised her bedraggled neighbours and let them in out of the cold wind.

Having received Stephenson Fountain's warning earlier that evening, the villagers of Damflask were not taken entirely unaware by the deluge which was about to strike their small settlement, although they were certainly not prepared for the violence of the flood. Joseph Hobson, the miller, heard the roar and congratulated himself on having taken such careful precautions to ensure that his precious stock of corn was safely stored. He could only indulge such thoughts, however, for a few minutes, for when the wall of water crashed into his mill the whole building was immediately demolished and its painstakingly stored contents washed far down the river. The flood then proceeded to deal in the same way with the bridge, The Barrel Inn and the three cottages behind it, of Joseph Walton, Henry Horsfield and Thomas Kirk.

It was only the Kirks, however, who, having listened to 'Sheffield Harry's' dismissal of any warnings of danger, were entirely unprepared. Neighbours standing outside in the lane shouted frantic warnings but, although he heard them, Harry refused to the end to believe that there was any real threat, and as he sat on the edge of his bed, pulling his socks on, the house crashed about him and carried him off. The surging water toyed with his body, smashing it against rocks and trees until 'Sheffield Harry' was unrecognisable.

Mrs. Kirk herself only made the narrowest of escapes. She heard the warning shouts and wasted no time in getting up and dressing. She fled straight down the stairs, out of the house and across the bridge in her night clothes before she remembered that her beloved pets, her cat and her dog, were still in the house. The roaring of the flood water was reaching a crescendo as she rushed back into her house. Within a few moments she reappeared carrying her dog under one arm and the cat under the other. She did not look back, but ran on over the bridge as, behind her, the cottage crashed into the waves. Nearby, at the wire mill, John King, Charles Platts and William Longden, together with their lad, John Ibbotson, were hard at work, to the accompaniment of the splashing of the water wheel and the grating of the cogs and wheels, heating steel rods and drawing it into thinner and thinner coils of wire which would eventually be used to make the framework for crinoline dresses. Intent as they were on watching the red-hot snaking metal it is certain that they had no warning of the flood until the powerful torrent tore away the end of the building in which they were working. The freezing water hissed and boiled for a moment as it extinguished the furnaces and cooled the steel and tossed the four workers to their death.

The death toll had now reached six, but all down the quiet valley dozens more ordinary working Sheffield people, either asleep in their beds or working in the mills, would add to this grim total within the next half hour, and hundreds of others, far away in the town who had never even heard the name Dale Dyke, would forfeit their lives before the next hour was up. On the floor of the valley, beside the river, stood twelve mills but few homes stood within the reach of the flood water, so until it reached Malin Bridge the deluge claimed few added victims. Had it not been that so many people were working in the mills all night it would have claimed far fewer.

The next mill to be reduced to ruins was Stacey Grinding Wheel, followed shortly afterwards by Storrs Bridge Rolling Mill and Storrs Bridge Forge together with the brickworks, kilns and boilers which also stood on this busy site. The churning water now carried along such a load of assorted bits and pieces that when the flood had subsided, about twenty minutes after the initial surge had struck, the scene resembled a major battlefield. Fully grown trees were uprooted or smashed and lay at unlikely and ugly angles. Boulders were strewn everywhere and sad, broken pieces of household debris littered the mud. Above all, there was the mud, deep, black and stinking.

The flood was now washing down towards Loxley Old Wheel, where, in the tilt forge, Joseph Denton, aged fourteen, and his eleven year old brother John, were working with Robert Banner. Their only warning was a noise like a rushing wind but they had no time to investigate before the doors were smashed open and they were sent sprawling into the freezing water. Banner was dashed against the chimney, which he desperately began to climb. From here he was able to work his way along the roof beams, always conscious of the foaming water below him, and out through a skylight. John Denton was a wiry lad, well used to clambering around in the local trees, and this stood him in good stead. Struggling in the water, he was just able to reach the shuttle pole which was used to control the speed of the water wheel and extended through the roof. Scrambling up the pole he reached a beam in the roof. He looked down, breathless and terrified, scanning the swirling water for his brother. He shouted his name, but there was no answer through the deafening roar. Joseph had not been so fortunate. The water had flung him out of the mill and carried him to his death.

Workmen pose beside the ruins of their wheel

Only a short distance further down the valley, where the road to Stannington crosses the river, was a busy group of buildings clustered around Rowell Bridge. The water from the large mill pond fed by the Loxley was used to turn the wheels of two large grinding hulls, which provided employment for around sixty people. As well as this, another smaller dam was fed by the Storrs Brook which joins the Loxley here. The water from this dam, which was on the hillside high above the buildings, powered a flour mill which occupied one of the buildings behind The Rowell Bridge Inn. As was usual in the local trades, the grinders here were self-employed and worked on a piece work basis, so it was not unusual for the grinders to work well into the night when there was water to turn the wheel, especially towards the weekend and payday! Sure enough, even on a night like this, the wheel was turning and the slapping leather belts and the creaking of the wooden gearing betrayed the presence of a solitary grinder, William Bradbury, still anxious to finish a few dozen pocket knife blades by the flickering candlelight. There was no one there to witness the fate of William, as the furious torrent of water crashed down onto the mill buildings, sweeping everything away. The stone bridge was bowled away and the Inn beside it flooded, although not destroyed. John Waters was able to shepherd his terrified family through the flour mill, into the hayloft and from there onto the hillside behind the house, from where they were able to witness the beer barrels being washed from his cellar and hear the screams of their two pigs, as the water carried them along.

Already the flood waters surged towards the next industrial hamlet, grouped around the Olive Paper Mill. Beside the mill dam here, with fine gardens, conservatories of choicest tender plants and lawns sweeping down to the waters of the attractive mill dam, stood one of the handsomest houses in the valley. Here lived Joshua Woodward, the owner of the paper mill. Fortunately for Mr. Woodward the house was not in the direct path of the flood as it swept round the bend, but it was invaded by the inky water, which left behind a stinking layer of mud and destroyed the carefully laid out gardens and wrecked the conservatories. The paper mill was one of the valley's most imposing buildings. Its three storeys stood proud above the grinding hull and the row of eight workers' cottages alongside it, but it did not withstand for long the battering of the flood water. Now new debris was added to the water's cargo; the rags, tubs, moulds and sieves used in paper making, as well as rolls and rolls of paper, which were carried along, unwinding, until they snagged and tore to hang like ragged flags on the boulders and broken trees which littered the path of the flood.

Even whilst the buildings at the Olive Wheel were still being tumbled by the flood, the surge was bearing down on the industrial hamlet clustered around Little Matlock mills, having between these two already demolished the Cliffe Wheel. The sides of the valley here are steep and rocky, and the full force of the torrent was directed straight at the group of buildings. The landlord of The Rock Inn, becoming aware of a roaring noise, looked up from the barrel that he was attending to and glanced down into the wooded valley below. At first he could not quite understand what he was seeing, but it only took him a fraction of a second to realise the danger of the white foaming wall that he could see rushing towards the buildings. "They'll all be killed! The dam's burst!" he shouted, loudly enough to bring Harrison Marshall and other neighbours out of their cottages.

Ruins of Wisewood Rolling Mill

The men stood transfixed, some of the few reluctant witnesses of the awesome power of the night's flood. Below them, in the valley bottom, another witness was having the shock his life. A cousin of young John Denton who was escaping with his life at the old wheel, having been stooped over his grindstone for the previous couple of hours, had just wandered over to the doorway, rubbing his tired eyes and stretching his cramped limbs, for a breath of air, when he saw the foaming wall of water thundering towards him. "John, Run! There's a flood!" was all that he had time to shout to his companion, John Bower, as he dashed up the hill towards his house and out of the water's path. But it's doubtful that Bower heard, above the screeching of the blade against the grindstone and the thundering din of water as it tore into the mill and smashed its walls, leaving him buried under the ruins.

Near the mill stood a row of five cottages, crosswise beside the river. The end cottage, fortunately uninhabited, took the full force of the flood and was immediately swept away, leaving only a chimneystack standing. In the next cottage, however, six people slept soundly in their beds. The house belonged to Daniel Chapman, who was proprietor of the mil,l and his brother Thomas lived next door. Daniel and his wife had only one son, Samuel, who was three, although Frederick, the six year old child of his brother Henry was also staying with them. The servant girl, Althea Hague and an apprentice, George Clay, were also in the house. Rather than demolishing the whole of this dwelling, the flood punched a gaping hole straight through it, sweeping away the entire contents, including the occupants, still in their beds.

In the next cottage, meanwhile, the water was smashing through the doors and windows, threatening to deal in a similar manner with the family of Thomas Chapman, Daniel's brother. Seeing that his son, William, was in dire danger of being swept out of the window by the rush of water now flowing through the house, Thomas grabbed hold of him and tried to pull him clear, at which point a beam crashed across his body and he involuntarily lost his grip on his son. There was a cry from the fourteen year old boy as the merciless water swept him out of his own bedroom window and bowled his body along for miles and miles. His grieving parents would spend the next few weeks scanning the white faces of dozens and dozens of likely sounding corpses whose discovery had been advertised in the local press, and who lay, awaiting identification, in the back room of many a public house along the Don Valley. They would eventually find his body in Swinton, beyond Rotherham. As for this night, Thomas turned from the horrific scene that he had been forced to witness and smashed a hole through the wall to give what assistance he could to his brother's family. He faced a scene of utter ruin, from which it only took a moment to correctly surmise the cruel fate of his relations. He turned back to the rest of his family and they all huddled, sobbing with cold and fear, in the corner of the bedroom for half an hour before Harrison Marshall was able to wade over and bring them all safely up the steep path to the warmth and shelter of The Rock Inn.

By the time that the water level had fallen enough for this rescue to take place, however, the crashing wave was wreaking havoc far below. In the mile and a half between Little Matlock and Malin Bridge the wheels of no less than seven mills

Damflask Wire Mill

Daniel Chapman's House

Remains of Tricket's Farm with the barns behind

42

gave employment to dozens of craftsmen. There was to be no work here for months to come. Instead the men and their families faced hardship and uncertainty. Other families, whose breadwinner had been drowned, faced the future with even greater dread but, at least, these would eventually receive some slight compensation payment. As the wave smashed its way down the narrow valley it obliterated Ashton Carr Wheel, destroyed the Glass tilt, smashed Harrison's tilt and forge, carrying away Joseph Gregory and Walter Booth who were still at work here, demolished Broadhead's Wheel, and tore down onto the Wisewood Scythe Wheel and Wisewood Rolling Mill, leaving nothing as it swept through but an eye-catching arrangement of cog wheels sticking from the mud and wreckage which would prove to be the focus of much attention from visitors to the stricken valley in the following few weeks, and which were to appear on many a souvenir photograph.

The death toll now stood at nineteen but, as the furious torrent now surged around the last bend and bore down on the still sleeping and unaware settlement at Malin Bridge, the events so far were but a minor precursor to the real horrors of the night. Beyond this point it was no longer possible to keep an accurate score of individual deaths for the water smashed rows of houses, cottages and mills almost simultaneously, sweeping away whole families and leaving none to identify the dead. The actual death toll would never be accurately recorded, a final indignity for those whose lives had been lived in poverty.

Not everyone in Malin Bridge was yet asleep. The night watchman, on his usual round, seeing a light from Ann Mount's small corner shop at the end of the row of twelve cottages beside the river, opened the door. "All's well, Mrs. Mount, I assume?" "Yes, everything's fine thank you. I'm going to lock up now, and then I'm for my bed. It's been a long day." "Aye, and it looks like being a long, cold night as well," joked the watchman. He was just about to wish the shopkeeper goodnight when he became conscious of a growing thundering noise. "What's that coming?" he said as Mrs. Mount came to join him at the door, never wishing to miss an event. "I think there's been a flood. Get inside quickly and lock your door securely. Quick as you can!" With that he left Mrs. Mount to secure her door and ran up the hill towards The Yew Tree Inn. As he ran the water was already beginning to foam around his heels. Had he been told later that he had stood transfixed for an hour watching the destruction of the village, the watchman wouldn't have been surprised, since time appeared to stand still, and the moving scene before him to unfold in slow motion. In fact the whole, terrible event was over in the space of little more than a few dreadful minutes. Even the terrifying din of the roaring water now faded from his consciousness as he became fully aware of the full horror of the spectacle before him, which was to be for ever imprinted on his mind's eye. At first he couldn't quite understand what his eyes could make out in the dark. Rather than water, the flood which now swooped onto the sleeping village appeared more like a foaming avalanche, the dirty white froth crashing over and over towards the first of the dwellings. It was as the great wave broke over the Tricket's farmhouse that he fully realised what he was seeing. For a moment he had the impression that the stone house, lights still shining from its upper windows, was floating on the crest of the wave but the lights were quickly extinguished as it crumbled below the black water, drowning all ten of the occupants. From nearby there was a screaming as the flood tore down a group of cottages near to the farmhouse, washing all six members of the Spooner family out. " Henry, save me!" screamed a woman's voice. But Henry Spooner and Charles Todd, a lodger, were themselves fighting for their lives in the surging water before being thrown up, coughing and spluttering, on the opposite bank of the Rivelin, which joins the Loxley here. None of the other family members were so fortunate.

The ruins of the Cleakum Inn

The wave swept round the bend, breaking over the cornmill and the row of twelve cottages, which the watchman knew as Bower's Buildings, which stood beside the river, and in which he had so recently been conversing with the shopkeeper, Mrs. Mount. The torrent crashed through the flimsy building tearing it apart, and the heartrending cries and screams of voices well known to him called out to the helpless watchman. The schoolmistress, Mrs. Etchell, the family of Joseph Crapper, the shoemaker, the Goddard family and the Jevissons, the Watsons and the shopkeeper, Edward Price, together with his two day old baby and the rest of the family and their lodgers and relations and, of course, Ann Mount herself were all now thrown into the swirling flood, crying out helplessly or being dragged down under the blackness. William Watson hung onto his wife and children for a little while until they were swept apart and he was flung against the debris which had collected against the side of the Widdowson's house. He clung onto the timber, shouting for help, and was relieved to see the bedroom window above him open and strong arms reach down to pull him to safety. Behind Bower's Buildings the house of Thomas Spooner toppled into the water drowning Thomas, his wife and her father and their seven children. Next for destruction were the public houses, The Stag and The Malin Bridge Inn, the scene of so much convivial company only a few short hours ago. The Stag, being nearer to the river, took the full force of the flood and crashed into the water, taking with it William and Anne Armitage, their five children and their grandmother, Eliza, as well as the servants and lodgers, ten people in all. Behind The Stag other cottages were tumbling. From one of these Greaves Armitage and his family were being swept to their deaths. The Malin Bridge Inn, 'The Cleakum', being set back a little, was not immediately destroyed. Instead the water tore the front wall out of the building leaving the interior exposed like a gruesome dolls house from which all the occupants, George Bisby, his wife and their five children, were plucked to their deaths. Already the avalanche was tearing on past the village, destroying the row of file cutters workshops below The Stag Inn and, as the water level began to subside, the watchman roused himself to run, together with many others who had been disturbed by the noise, towards the scene of destruction.

The ruins of the village of Malin Bridge

He recognised faces of other horrified onlookers as he hurried to give whatever help he could, including the face of Joseph Crownshaw who had run full tilt from Wisewood Works to warn his sister Elizabeth, the servant girl at The Stag. But there was nothing that they could do. They stood in a group, peering into the thick, dark water, holding their hands over their faces against the putrid stench which it gave off. The bodies of ninety-four villagers now swirled in the eddies, were bowled along in its wake or were thrown up in the thick mud with the other debris. Having ripped through the village of Malin Bridge, the wall of foaming water was tearing down the Limerick Wheel and William Bethel, who was spending the night softening the steel in the furnace ready for it to be drawn into the wire for rich ladies' crinolines the next morning, was either drowned or shattered by the enormous explosion which ripped apart the four red-hot furnaces as the water which surged into them suddenly turned to steam. The flood quickly covered the half mile below Malin Bridge and reached Hill Bridge, where the old road down the hill from Walkley was lined with about twenty cottages right to the river side, all of them laying directly in the path of the oncoming torrent. It was not long before the families presently sleeping here would become conscious of the water rising in the bedroom or of the sickening crash as part of their house disintegrated.

Henry Whittles, in a cottage near the bridge, woke suddenly with a sickening feeling of fear. There was a crashing noise downstairs. Someone must be breaking into the house! He bravely jumped out of bed and set off to investigate. As he set foot on the stairs however, he found himself standing in rising water. Still bemused, but now acutely aware of the danger, his thoughts turned to the protection of his wife and five children, the baby only nine days old. On one side of the small, poorly- furnished room his wife lay on the bed with the two youngest children, the other children occupying what was little more than a mattress against the opposite wall. "Get up, quickly!" exclaimed Henry, bundling his wife and baby out of the bed across to the other side of the room. Turning back to the bed, he only had time to snatch the other child up and fling him over his head onto the mattress before the outside walls and the part of the room holding the bed slid away into the blackness, leaving the whole family clinging onto the tiny refuge of the corner of the room hanging above the swirling water. The water rose even higher and the children now had to stand to keep their heads above it. Henry Whittles hung onto them for grim death to prevent them from being swept away like the other poor souls who floated past them in the water, but whom they were powerless to help. A whole endless hour passed in this way before the terrified and freezing family recognised a familiar voice. A neighbour, George Allen, a grinder by trade, was shouting to his companions in the search. "There's no one here. It looks as though the whole family's lost." From somewhere Henry Whittles found the strength to shout back. "No, we are safe. We're here in the corner." It was then the work of only a few minutes to hand the children down into the safe hands of the many friends and neighbours who wished to share in such a dramatic and unlikely rescue.

But such dramatic events are unusual only on everyday occasions. On this night they were commonplace. In house after house such extraordinary scenes were being enacted. Near to the Whittles' house Robert Graham was having his own battle to save his family from death. It was taking all his strength to hold his family on the bed while the flood water swirled it around the room, threatening to tip them all to their deaths at any moment. At the Mason's Arms nearby the eight year old niece of the publican, William Pickering, was woken by a loud noise, but felt too sleepy to get up from her bed in the top storey room to see what was happening. She heard her aunt and her twin sister both go downstairs and call for help but then, when everything went quiet again, she simply went back to sleep. And that's how

'The whole house was swept away, except the corner on which I had placed my wife and five children, on the little bed.'

Henry Whittles

the rescuers would find her the next day, safely asleep, unaware that all the rest of her family had been drowned.

In one of the cottages in Bower's Row, a little higher up the hill, William Crookes was so frightened by the terrifying scene that lay before him when he looked out of his bedroom window that he jumped out onto the flooded road below, receiving injuries from which he was to die the next morning. Meanwhile, on the other side of the bridge which was smashed in the flood's first impact, the events were no less dramatic and tragic. Beside the road stood the newly built three storey monstrosity called Brick Row, consisting of twelve houses at the front and twelve back-to-back with them. Like most others built in the town at the time they were built with greater consideration for the profits of the builders than the comfort of the occupants, and the structure was certainly not designed to survive a battering by millions of gallons of pounding water. The flood water now struck the end of the row, smashing the first two houses and leaving the interiors exposed. As it did so, Richard Snape in the top bedroom quickly smashed a hole through both the ceiling and the roof and sat high above the terrible scene on the windy ridge, as the other nine occupants of the house, including eight of the Dyson family, were washed to their deaths. Here Richard could not feel safe because the foaming water was buffeting the flimsy building so much that the whole thing shook. The water was continuing to rise. It was now over sixteen feet above the level of the road. Other residents of the block were being drowned in their beds or washed out of their windows; the Atkinson children, the Drabbles and the Turners.

In the house adjoining the Dysons, Joseph Hides was making his way by candlelight down the stairs to investigate the cause of the shattering noise when he stumbled on the broken staircase and only just saved himself from falling into the water below. In trying to save himself, however, he lost his grip on the candle he was holding, stumbled and broke one of his fingers. Turning back in pain he could now hear the terrified screams of his family as the house shook. Reaching the bedroom, he wrenched off a bedpost and set about hacking a hole in the wall to the next house. Once through into the adjoining bedroom still none of the neighbours felt safe so they continued to break down the walls into the next four houses, collecting with them the terrified occupants. In the middle of the block there collected a most unlikely assembly of some thirty neighbours in one small room, all still dressed in only their night clothes and screaming and crying with fear. In one of their houses the flood water stopped the clock at twenty seven minutes past twelve.

Had Richard Snape's vision been keen enough his eyes might have been able to pick out one particularly strange sight amongst all the others in the darkness. As the water surged on past Brick Row it destroyed nearby cottages, in one of which lived Joseph Chapman, a retired tailor. As the flood level rose, and his belongings were carried away, Joseph had the presence of mind to climb into a large wooden box, in which he floated about until the water went down. Since, however, he had lost all his clothes, he squatted in the box until, terribly embarrassed, he was discovered later and rescued.

In another minute or two the flood reached Hillsborough Bridge, then, as now, a busy spot. Beside the strong stone bridge, which was damaged but surprisingly remained standing, the toll house on the Wadsley and Langset turnpike was swept away, and with it old Thomas Winter, the keeper. In the nearby police station Inspector Thomas Smalley and his wife were roused by the screams from the prisoner in the lockup below, who was awaiting an appearance in court after having attempted to take his own life by jumping into the river! The police officer quickly rescued the man, now up to his armpits in the water, and went out to help others as he could.

The valley here widens out and on the left hand side is more level towards Hillsborough Park. Here the water slowed and vast amounts of debris were deposited. The most amazing of these was a whole brick house which came to rest beside the bridge before collapsing into the river. Much of the heavy burden of flotsam carried along by the rushing tide was now deposited in this shallower backwater. The furniture, machinery, boots, wire, bedding and bodies, all were dumped indiscriminately into the thick black mud which lapped up against the elegant kitchen garden walls of Mr. Dixon's home, Hillsborough Hall.

On the right hand side of the river below the bridge the new stone built barracks presented an imposing sight, its thick tall walls towering over the more flimsy, brick built cottages and mills, but even these walls were no match for the power of this flood, and the sentry on duty that night must be excused for abandoning his post and fleeing to higher ground. The first that Sergeant Foulds, the regiment's paymaster, knew of the impending disaster was when he and his wife heard a tremendous noise outside the room. "The windows are being smashed. It must be the wind," shouted his wife above the din, but as they leaped out of bed they found themselves waist deep in water which was rushing in through their ground floor window. The couple had only recently been posted to Sheffield and had no idea what could be happening. As the sergeant looked out of the window he became even more confused, for the strong boundary wall was gone and sweeping past was a torrent carrying the bodies of men, women and children and debris of all kinds. "The world is breaking up!" he cried in utter confusion and made his way to the door to escape with his wife and children. At first it would not open because of the pressure of water against it but he eventually forced it open and rescued his wife and baby, which was by this time floating in its cot. Unfortunately the door closed behind him and the water pressure inside the room was so great that he was unable to force his way back in to rescue the two other children, five year old Isabella and three year old John, who were trapped and drowned on the other side of the door in the flooded bedroom.

A little way below Hillsborough Bridge the river passed through the busy village of Owlerton where Mr. Hawksley's Rolling Mill was destroyed and his garden flooded. A watchman on his rounds, hearing the thunderous noise was attempting to outrun the flood but the water caught up with him as he reached Mr. Hawksley's garden wall. He climbed up a gas lamp and clung on, up to his neck in water. Mr. Hawksley, hearing his cries for help, came out and helped him into the house, none the worst for his soaking. The Shakespeare Inn and The Blue Ball were damaged, as was Marshall's Paper mill. In the nearby cottage of Mr. Shaw the lodger, Mr. Ashton, was having the fright of his life as the body of a man, entirely naked except for a torn shirt held only to his wrist, swept into the house on the rising tide. It was later identified as the remains of Joseph Goddard from Malin Bridge. In other nearby cottages Joseph Dean and the Turton family were being swept to their deaths.

Row of cottages with one side entirely washed away, at Bacon Island.

Down the Don to Sheffield

The flood waters were now washing across the broad meadows through which the Loxley meanders to join the Don. The glinting moonlight cast a fitful gleam across this scene; a very different scene from the same charming picture painted by the local artist, Edward Price, only the previous August. As he sat in front of his easel on the hillside above Wardsend on the far side of the River Don on that sunny Sunday afternoon he had felt in fine spirits. Above him the skylarks sang, around him the insects hummed, and below him the two rivers wound their picturesque way across the Birley Meadows, where cows grazed contentedly and reapers busied themselves cutting and stacking the harvest into sheaves. The weather had been kind and the patient heavy horses stood waiting to lead the heavily-loaded wagons back to the farmsteads. Weirs and channels cut across the loops of the rivers, directing the sluggish flow towards mills whose wheels churned the steadily flowing water. The sound of children's shouts and laughter drifted towards the artist as he worked, as happy family groups enjoyed the country air beyond the smoky town, picnicking on the grass beside the riverside tracks.

The Valley of the Don   *Edward Price 1863*

But on this night the same scene was frightful. A surge of water was now sweeping over the fields and meadows and washing up against the iron gates of Wardsend cemetery at the foot of the hillside. Many of the bodies of the flood's unfortunate victims swirled along in the churning, muddy water. Now, surely, the flood should have spent its power, and the accumulated water, steadily spreading across the meadowland, should safely drain away. Not at all. Having wreaked havoc down the length of the Loxley, the filthy water was now gathering itself for a second onslaught towards the unaware sleeping town. Hundreds of poor Sheffield folk were about to experience an event which, should they survive it, would make a permanent mark on their lives, as the pent up water swept down the valley towards them.

The wave was now funnelled down the Don Valley, announcing its arrival by crashing through the gable end of Marchington and Makin's file works. The fifteen foot high wall of water ripped through the factory, tossing in its wake huge pieces of masonry which it had excavated from the riverbed, iron railings from the riverside walkway, anvils and machinery from the workshops and a thirty foot long boiler, on top of which William Simpson, who had been working through the night, clung for his life. It proved impossible for him to hang on for long, and after a few more yards he was flung to his death with a terrible shriek. The huge boiler was tossed along for another mile.

At the far end of the works opposite Hillfoot Bridge, stood The Fairfield Inn. Beside the inn stood a row of houses whilst to the front, between the river and the railway embankment, there was the level area laid out with neatly tended allotments and pleasure gardens, dotted here and there with a motley variety of small brick buildings. These had been intended originally as little more than shelter for the pigs, rabbits and pigeons on which the poorer people depended. Now, however, many of them provided accommodation for the poor families themselves. All the locals were well known to Matilda Mason, the landlady of The Fairfield, who was now thankfully settling down for the night after a busy evening in the bar. Gradually she became aware of a growing noise, which at first she took to be a steam train travelling towards Sheffield at an unaccustomed time. But the noise grew to become a rumbling shriek which filled the room and started to vibrate the whole building. Crossing fearfully to the window Matilda could at first make out nothing to explain the uproar but then, as the din reached a deafening crescendo, everything happened at once.

She could now see wild water rushing around the building and sweeping across the gardens. The torrent rose higher and higher and in no time was level with her bedroom. She realised with terror that she had no means of escape and so was forced to be an unwilling spectator to horrific scenes now unfolding before her, without being able to do anything to warn her sleeping customers below. No sooner had the occupants of the garden houses roused themselves to investigate the cause of the roaring noise than they found themselves floundering in the freezing water which continued to rise in their insubstantial homes. Most, like the five members of the Kay family, had no escape route and no time to think and were quickly drowned inside their house. Others, such as the Midwoods, were washed out of the house to splash and splutter in the foaming water before being dragged under. Yet others clutched desperately onto floating bits of furniture and branches. Most only prolonged their agony before they too were wrenched away to their deaths, but a very lucky few, like Joel Midwood, managed to cling on long enough to be washed onto a heap of debris from which he managed to scramble to safety, completely exhausted. Only later was he to discover that all the rest of his family were now dead. Here and there the flimsy houses tumbled into the water as great chunks of machinery or timber collided with them. Mrs. Mason watched as families climbed out and clung desperately onto their roofs or anything which might keep them above the water level. Mrs. Bennet found the strength to climb into a cherry tree. The tree swayed in the waves and Mrs. Bennet screamed before being flung to her death. Nearby William Wright was encouraging his wife and three terrified children onto the roof of their little house. The water swirled round as they huddled there, all quite naked in the freezing night. Part of the building fell away with a crash. Miraculously however, enough of the house still stood to support the roof and the family shivered there throughout the night until they could be rescued at last, early the next morning.

As the wall of water swept on, other families attempting similar escapes were not to be so fortunate. At the far end of the gardens, at the bottom of Neepsend Lane, a row of poor whitewashed cottages stood beside the river. In one of these cramped cottages lived John and Sarah Gannon with their six children. Henry, the eldest was eleven, whilst little Margaret, the latest baby, had been born four months previously. John had managed to shepherd the whole family onto the roof where all eight now clung to each other beside the chimney. Suddenly the house juddered, the children wailed, and the whole building appeared to lift on the wave before breaking apart and collapsing into the black water which closed mercilessly over the whole scene, extinguishing the cries of the family for ever. Nearby, the water rushed into the cellar of a house where the three Coggan children were sleeping. They were alone. Their parents had left them to attend a funeral in Wakefield so there was no one to hear their plaintive wails as the flood poured in on them.

Now the flood waters had reached the built-up edge of the town of Sheffield itself. From Neepsend Lane the terraces of houses lined the narrow streets, cheek by jowl with factories and pubs and, as the tidal wave of filthy water cascaded along the streets, it sought out and filled the passageways which led into the courtyards, cutting off the only escape route for the families who lived around them. In a cottage in just such a courtyard lived the family of Thomas Albert, a skinner who worked at the nearby tannery. The time was shortly past one o'clock when the rushing water roused Mr. Albert. Coming downstairs to investigate he found the ground floor already awash and the level rising. He hurried back and shouted upstairs to the other members of his family, who were already out of their beds. Clutching his three year old son he shouted, "Hold tightly round my neck and don't let go. John, Mary Jane, you hold tightly onto each other and your mother, there's been a flood, we'll have to all wade out." They got downstairs but as they made their way to the door it burst open and Catherine Albert, his wife, screamed, "We're all going to drown in this hole!" and sure enough she was swept off her feet by the force of the flood surging into the room. "Hold on, Catherine," shouted Thomas as, pushing through the water, he reached a flight of stone steps in the yard on which he placed the child out of reach of the water. Quickly he turned back to rescue his wife and other children. As he struggled back across the yard, however, he was struck by swirling timbers and falling masonry and he had only a fleeting glimpse of his family choking and sobbing as they were overcome by the water.

In the same yard their neighbour, Mrs. Peters, was also struggling to get her four children to safety out of their house. Desperately they cried and clutched one another but little Christopher was only two and Julia only four and they were quickly engulfed by the freezing, buffeting waves. Eight year old Jane managed to hang on for a few more moments before she was also wrenched from her mother's grasp. But Mrs. Peters was now within the reach of Thomas Albert who grabbed her and her remaining child and together they struggled back into his own house and fell, exhausted, on the stairs, the only survivors of both families. Interspersed between the dismal rows of dirty red brick houses stood the high walls and elaborate gateways of the various factories which provided the people with their meagre living. As the flood water invaded these premises further havoc and mayhem ensued. It rushed into the red-hot retorts of the Neepsend Gas Works and immediately the brown liquid frothed, hissed and boiled and clouds of acrid smoke rose from its surface. Tons of coke were added to the flood's burden and, amidst the smoke and rising vapour, the tall factory chimney toppled into the foam. The water now explored the stinking tan pits of the two local tanneries, Mills and Fawley's, adding their unspeakable contents to the mixture. It surged into the local breweries, smashing the vats and carrying off malt, barley, beer and barrels, which bobbed and danced along before being smashed.

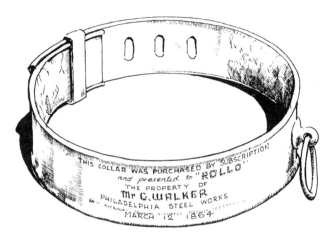

The brass collar of 'Rollo', now in Sheffield City Museum's collection. What Rollo did to deserve such recognition is not recorded.

On the opposite side of the river, the wall of water was now sweeping towards Bacon Island. On his usual nightly patrol, the neighbourhood policeman, P.C. John Thorpe, had just reached Hillfoot, the point across the river opposite to the island in the Don. Pulling his heavy cloak tightly round himself against the biting cold wind, he became aware of a growing, unaccountable, roaring sound. Immediately alert, he turned to look up the river and thus became one of the few that night to witness the alarming sight, some two hundred yards away, of the front of the wave pounding over the allotments and the Victoria Gardens. His eyes swept to the right, downstream, in front of the flood, and he didn't take long to deduce that the residents of Bacon Island, on their spit of land between the two arms of the river, were in imminent danger. Military service in India and the Crimea had prepared the policeman well, and, although he wasn't as young as he used to be, he sprang quickly into action, pounding down the road towards the island, hollering a warning with all his might and blaring on his whistle, although by now the noise of the crashing water reverberated through the night air, drowning any such puny human attempts to raise the alarm. "James! James Sharman! Get out! The river's flooding", screamed the policeman above the din as he beat on the door of the first house on the island, the Shuttle House, where the shuttle keeper, James Sharman lived with his family. The family were well known to P.C. Thorpe from regularly meeting them on his daily patrol. By the time that his frantic hammering got a response, and the head and shoulders of James Sharman appeared at the bedroom window, the policeman was already up to his waist in the water which flowed all round the house. "What on earth's happening! Has one o' t'dams gone?" the shuttleman shouted down. Since his job was to control the flow of water through the sluices to the mills on the island he was only too well aware of the danger of one of the mill dams bursting, but a flood on this scale was beyond his comprehension. "I don't know what's caused it, but we've got to be quick, it's rising fast! Throw the children down. I'll catch 'em."

James Sharman disappeared from the window and reappeared a few moments later, clutching his terrified daughter. At first she clung, sobbing, around his neck, refusing to let go, but eventually, with a scream, she allowed herself to be thrown down into the waiting policeman's arms. Quickly he waded the fifty yards to a house at the bottom of George Street, where the occupants, who by this time had been roused by the noise, readily took in the terrified child. P.C. Thorpe was already hurrying back to the Sharman's house, where the next sobbing child was waiting at the window to be rescued. In all the policeman made the trip backwards and forwards, bearing his precious loads, eight times before finally helping the children's father from the stricken house and across the bridge to safety. "Run! Run for your life!" he shouted above the din to Sharman, sensing that the house couldn't stand against the battering for much longer and, sure enough, as they reached the safety of the main road both house and bridge crumbled and were swallowed into the great sheet of water. As John Thorpe stood trembling with cold and near exhaustion, a concerned group of local people were now gathering round the two men, some of them still hastily pulling clothes around themselves. Seeing the Shuttle House sliding into the water many of them feared the worst, thinking that all the family of their neighbour was still inside. "Oh the poor souls! Those poor little children!" "It's alright. They're safe. This brave policeman saved them all! I saw it all. He deserves a medal, he does!" Someone held up a lantern to illuminate Thorpe's tired face. General congratulations followed until another of the crowd piped up, "Here, let him get in to get warm and dry. He'll catch his death like that! Here come wi' me. You can get warm by mi' fire and I'll make yer a nice hot cup of tea."

But what had become of the other families stranded on the flooded island the group could only guess at until the water level subsided enough for them to carefully edge across the slippery top of the shuttle gates. Stepping carefully through the thick, stinking mud, picking their way over and between an assortment of wreckage, they made their way slowly towards the cottages at the other end of the island, past the more imposing home of William Howe, the electroplate and Britannia metal manufacturer whose works were on Lambert Street. The door stood ajar, forced open by the pressure of the water which had invaded the house and ruined the expensive contents, the books, piano and music, the engravings and the walnut furniture. But candles burning in the upstairs rooms indicated to the rescuers that the family, at least, were safe. The swaying lanterns were a welcome sight to the residents of the row of cottages at the end of the island who, although they were badly shaken, were safe, and called to the rescuers from their bedroom windows. "We're all safe here, thank you", shouted Mrs. Mappin from the first window, "But I don't know about Mr. and Mrs. Wright next door." The group made their way round to the neighbouring cottage, only to find that the end wall had been completely carried away. "Is Mr. Wright there?" called Mrs Mappin, "Only I heard him knocking and then there were a loud crash." But, although a flickering candle still burned in the wrecked bedroom, there was no sign of life in the ruined building. "I'll get up there and see if I can see anyone. Maybe someone's hurt", said one of the group, not believing himself that this could be possible. He scrambled around in the debris to find a suitable length of wood which could be hoisted up against the wall. This done, the young man, assisted by the others, was soon climbing up this makeshift ladder into the room. Almost immediately he gave a shout, "There's a child here! She's still asleep in the bed!" Gently he lowered the still sleepy little girl to the upraised hands of the waiting companions. "Where are your mama and papa?" they asked when she was safe. "They have gone out of the window" replied the bemused little child, rubbing her sleepy eyes.

Detail from   *'A Flood' by Milais*

There is nothing to suggest that such an event ever occurred in Sheffield.

The wave was now rushing through narrow streets of densely packed, overcrowded houses, jennels and alleyways, this way and that, and so much was happening that the scene became one of utter confusion. Around every low-lying yard, in every ground-floor room, similar horrific events were being acted out minute by minute, as the eight foot high wall of water surged on regardless, smashing down walls of the strongest materials and sweeping away the hovels of the poor in a dark, deadly tide. In no two places, however, were the events and experiences quite the same.

The three young men, wrapped in their heavy working jackets, scarves, flat caps and clogs who were at this time crossing the river over Ball Street Bridge on their way to work on the night shift at the Lion Steel Works on the opposite bank, were to be some of the few, like P.C. Thorpe, who actually witnessed the approaching wall of water and survived to tell the tale. They were in good spirits, having spent most of the previous evening in the bar of The Hallamshire Hotel. "He were cheatin' I tell yer. He can't have been playing fair to win so much off me on shove ha'penny board!" complained one of the trio. His friends scoffed. They'd heard it all before. "Hey! What's that noise?" "I don't know. It's coming from up t'river." They stood in the middle of the bridge gazing into the dark space where the river ran between tall factory back walls. As the fearful rumble grew to a terrible pitch the foaming wave swept into view round a bend about two hundred yards from the men. They stood transfixed and speechless for a second as it churned towards them, its miscellaneous cargo, great pieces of timber, furniture, boilers and bodies, both human and animal, rolling along in its foaming wake. Even as they gathered themselves to turn and run the wave had already covered half of the distance towards them and, as they reached the end of the bridge, they were struck from their right and swept off their feet by a wave flowing along Cornish Street. The water carried them along towards Shalesmoor but, fortunately, the level was not too deep here and they managed to keep their heads above water for most of the time before being thrown up, coughing and spluttering, against the wall of The Hallamshire Hotel.

Mr Wagstaffe, an elderly man who lodged at the hotel, heard shouting and, looking out of his window, was amazed to see three men clinging to his windowsill as a tide of brown water flowed all around. He reached out but, to the men's consternation, hadn't the strength to pull them in. "Quickly! Get help! We can't hold on much longer!" they implored and to their great relief, within a few seconds, the familiar face of Charles Staniforth, the burly landlord, appeared at the window. "Right lads. Don't fret. We'll soon have you out o' there," he reassured the exhausted friends, and he quickly fetched a rope, tied one end to the bedpost and threw the other through the window. With this the three were able to drag themselves to safety.

Across the river, at the Eagle Works on Mowbray Street, Sarah Jane Green and her aunt were woken by the screaming of pigs. Her aunt lifted the blind to see the water rolling wave upon wave towards them and let out a great shriek. "Oh, John, wake up. The world's at an end!" "No, surely not. It can't be," replied the girl's uncle as he sat up. "I'll go and see what's happening." He went down the stairs but was soon back to report that the water level was up to the third step. Just then the gas light spluttered and went out and the family were thrown into complete darkness. Uncle John managed to find and light a stub of candle. Sarah's aunt was so terrified that the eleven year old found herself trying to comfort her in the dimly flickering candlelight. "If the water comes any higher I think we will have to climb out onto the roof," said the uncle, but when he again gingerly went down to investigate the water had gone down a step and the danger was past for them. They lay down again in their beds but after such an experience any idea of sleep was impossible, and they lay there, longing for a cup of tea.

As the flood now raced down the narrow streets the yellow pools of light beneath the street lamps were extinguished one by one and the invading water, now flooding into the tightly packed houses, ensured that any living thing unable to reach higher ground, or to escape to the relative safety of an upper room, had little chance of survival. Dennis Mc'Loughlin and his donkey slept soundly in adjoining rooms of a shed in a yard in Dun Street. Both were drowned as the water quickly filled the building to its roof. In nearby Long Croft, Christopher Calton, his wife and his four year old nephew were all drowned in their downstairs room despite frantic attempts to escape. Over the road Priscilla Willett was being swept away to her death having lost her footing whilst trying to follow her father out of the flooded yard, and Mrs. Ryder was attempting to get her own son and daughter to safety, the three of them clinging together for dear life as the wave buffeted them down the street. Reaching a lamppost they hung on to it, oblivious to the shouts and entreaties of the neighbours who were powerless spectators from their bedroom windows. The current dragged at their heavily sodden clothes and little Bob could hold on no longer. "Oh mother!" came the desperate and forlorn cry as he was carried from her grasp. But now his mother was struggling to save herself and her daughter for the water was up around her neck. Having exhausted her strength the poor woman was forced to release her grip on the post and the pair were swept along screaming. Mercifully the wave threw them up against the wall of The King William Inn into which they could be pulled to safety through a window.

On the opposite, eastern side of the river, a particularly high proportion of the courtyards accommodated sties, sheds and stabling for an extraordinary menagerie of domestic animals; horses, pigs, cattle, donkeys, fowls and rabbits, on which the precarious livelihoods of the locals depended. Such livestock had little chance of escape and were drowned in amazingly high numbers. On Harvest lane the pigs of Mr. Clayton, the grocer, were swept away, whilst in the same locality Mr. Batty lost five and Henry Frost and Mr. Hinchliffe six each, their contribution towards the total of 258 pigs whose bloated corpses needed to be disposed of in the days which followed. Nearby ten valuable horses, on which the business of Faulkner and Co., the carriers, depended, were all lost. In nearby Orchard Street the widow Twigg lost the only way of supporting her family as her six cows drowned, and back across Ball Street Bridge the landlord of The Boatman Inn, standing in the shadow of James Dixon's great cutlery factory, could only watch from the upper window as the flood wrecked his stables and carried off his two horses and eight pigs.

The flood level at Ball Street had now risen higher than the bridge parapets and for a while the water flowed right over in a continuous sheet until, with a great shudder and groan, the structure suddenly gave way under the battering from the tons and tons of timber and machinery which were thrown up against its arches, completely blocking them. The released fury of this pent up wave bore down on Kelham Island, directly ahead. Like Bacon Island, Kelham Island, a narrow strip of land a few hundred yards long, stands in the middle of the river, below Ball Street Bridge, and the full force of the great wave was directed straight at the island by the curving stone steps of the ancient weir across the river bed. In times of normal river flow the weir performed the essential service of diverting some of the river's flow along the channel which had cut this piece of land off from the rest of Sheffield for the last four hundred years. This water was put to work turning the wheels of the mills which straddled its channel. Like Bacon Island, Kelham Island was also crowded with cottages built against grimy mill and factory walls, tall chimneys, furnaces of molten steel, wrought iron factory gates and tiny yards enclosing stables and pig sties.

As Ball Street Bridge crashed into the waves the havoc hit the sharp end of Kelham Island, and the night's terrible events seemed to be reaching a dramatic crescendo. Tall brick and stone walls came crashing down, riverside mills and cottages slid into the wave, red-hot furnaces exploded, tall chimneys toppled, fires suddenly flared up and above all, the deafening roar of the furious water all but drowned the wails and screams of stricken people and animals that floundered in its wake. The factory belonging to Wheatman and Smith, the saw makers, stood at the end of the island and was quickly demolished. Their huge grindstones were bowled along by the torrent, which then rolled over the works of Crowley's, iron founders, whose workers, for the first time in months, had finished their work early and left at ten. Two delivery horses, in their stable in the yard, were spooked by the noise. One of them, kicking and rearing to escape, forced his head through a window and was unable to release himself as the water struck, whilst the other managed to survive by standing on his rear legs with his fore legs resting on the body of his mate.

At the next works the sleeping watchman was roused by the commotion. Suddenly fully alert to the terrible danger, he screamed a warning and raced across the works yard towards the open doors of the mill. The team of men with long handled tongs were drawing snaking lengths of red hot, glowing steel between the iron rollers with a deft, almost casual skill from long practice. "Get out, the river's rising. The island's flooding!" shouted the watchman, but by this time the men needed no warning as water flowed through the open door and hissed across the hot iron floor. They came rushing out, wading through the rising water, towards the factory gate, only to find that, for some reason, it was locked. "Good God, we'll all be drowned, where the hell's the key?" "There's no time to look for that. Here, climb up on t'roof." So, frantically grabbing for any hand or foothold, the men scrambled up onto the beams above the factory floor. In doing so one of them knocked over a barrel of light oil and the spreading pool was quickly ignited from a redhot steel ingot which had been hurriedly dropped. Tall blue flames now danced over the surface of the swirling water and the men in the roof beams held their breath in fear as they considered whether they were going to suffer death by fire or by water! But the fire burned down and the beams held firm and the men clung on to witness the chaotic scene below. One of the workmen gave a loud gasp and pointed, "That's my bed! I left my wife and children asleep in it at Malin Bridge." The next few hours would reveal the grim fact that his wife, two children and his father had been carried off.

Tucked tightly against Crowley's wall at the southern end of the island were three small cottages. The three families who lived in these cottages, the Hills, the Clarkes and the Eatons, had been roused by the noise and commotion over the wall and as faces now appeared from the relative safety of their upstairs windows water began to flood into the communal yard below. For the Hills this was only one of many recent broken nights sleep. For the past weeks they had been up almost hourly to tend to their three children, now turning fitfully in their little beds in the fever of smallpox. The Eatons, like most families, kept a pig in a sty in the yard. This pig was an especially fat animal, enormously prized by the family who had lovingly reared it, coaxed it, scratched its great back with a stick and fed it with every available scrap for months, anticipating the bacon, ham and black pudding that would keep the family going through the following winter. It is only this which makes it understandable that John Eaton, seeing his most precious possession squealing for its life as its sty rapidly filled with filthy water, determined to take action. After all the loss of the pig could well be the final straw to land the destitute family in the dreaded workhouse. "I must save t'pig!" he shouted over his shoulder as he rushed out of the bedroom, down the stairs.

Whilst his wife watched anxiously from the window John waded across the flooding yard to the animal's shelter. He tried to coax the pig out. He tried to push and poke the pig out. But it refused to budge. His heart thumping and breathing heavily, Mr. Eaton paused for breath and became aware that, above the din, his wife and neighbours were screaming at him and pointing to something beyond the wall."Get out John! Save yourself! Leave it!" is all that he could make out before the full force of the flood hit the wall, bringing it crashing down, engulfing the sty and carrying off the screaming pig and dashing its owner ferociously against the opposite wall. "Help! Save me!" he gasped as the foaming water swirled round the yard. "Hold on John! I'm coming!" shouted his wife, but it was too late and the water tore him from the wall and swept him to his death, watched by his horrified neighbours. To compound their horror Clarke and Hill now saw the figure of Keziah Eaton, John's wife, struggling out of the door below them. "I'm coming John! Hang on!" she cried, not realising that her husband was beyond rescue, and the two shocked observers got no chance to shout a warning, but had to watch helplessly as the water swept Keziah off her feet and her long heavy skirts dragged her under and away down the mill race to join her husband.

On the western side of the river the six foot wave roared through the narrow streets, towards the sinister dark ugly mass of the Workhouse, a four storey converted cotton mill, standing on Kelham Street, which seemed to loom over the surrounding cottages and factories. As with a number of local buildings the sewers of the workhouse discharged directly into the river so there were tunnels running from the building directly to the riverbank, enabling the rising water to rush through with enough pressure to force up the wooden floors of the ground floor wards, which served as accommodation to the women lunatics and to children suffering from measles, diphtheria and smallpox. There was no way that these poor people could have had any idea why their beds should so suddenly begin to rise and float about as the stinking water rose higher and higher. All they could do was to set up a fearful shrieking and wailing which disturbed the sleep of Miss Rebecca Day, the matron. On hearing the din Miss Day quickly threw a cloak around herself, lit a candle and hurried to rouse the Master, James Wescoe. But the master was already out of his bed. "What on earth is going on?" she demanded, on meeting him on the stairs. "I have no idea, ma'am. I think that the water tanks on the roof must have burst," he replied. The two of them made their way to the wards on the ground floor, making sure that all the inmates on the upper floors were securely locked in to prevent anyone being injured in the rising tide of panic. Realising that the children on the ground floor across the yard were in great danger, Mr. Wescoe recruited a group of twenty or so men who waded across the flooded yard, at no small danger to themselves, and brought all the terrified children to safety on the upper floors. Thanks to their bravery and Wescoe's quick thinking no lives were lost at the Workhouse, but the institution's part in the story was far from over, for it was to be here that many of the bodies would be brought the following day, and the grim process of identification begun, and it was to be the Workhouse which was to provide vital shelter for the next weeks for two hundred people who had lost their homes.

In one of the meagre cottages facing the high blank wall of the Workhouse, across the narrow lane still called Cotton Mill Walk, the Johnson family were fighting for their lives. As their room filled with water they were forced against the window and their desperate faces could be seen as they frantically battered on the pane to attract attention. Fortunately their cries were heard by two policemen who came wading against the strong current to reach them. They wasted no time in smashing the window and pulling to safety the children, their parents and the lodger. They all made their way towards The King William Inn on Green Lane where they were made as comfortable as possible with other refugees who had taken shelter here from the night's terrors.

The six children of the Wells family had been left to face the unexpected deluge alone in their little cottage nearby. As usual, their mother had left them to collect from their father the bunches of watercress that he had been gathering during the week from the clear Pennine streams miles away, so that she could sell them for a penny a bunch at the Saturday market in Sheffield. It was now, as the flood water was at its height at about one o'clock, that she returned only to find that she couldn't get anywhere near her cottage for the swirling water. In frustration and distress she flung the basket of cress into the wave and the leaves spread and bobbed along the surface. The group of onlookers tried to comfort her and prevent her from wading in but through her shrieks and sobs they discovered that two of the children, her thirteen year old son and his three year old sister, had been left sleeping in the downstairs room, and that they, at least, must surely have been drowned. The agonising wait for the water to subside is all too easily imagined and all must secretly have imagined that there was little hope of finding any of the children alive

Workmen search for their tools in the ruins of their mill.

despite their reassuring words to the frantic mother. As the level gradually dropped the crowd inched forwards down the devastated lanes, slipping on the thick layer of glistening mud and holding their cloaks in front of their faces against the nauseous stink. At last Mrs Wells got within calling distance of the cottage and waded through the slime to shout to the children. To her immense joy and relief the frightened faces of the children who had been sleeping upstairs appeared at the window. "Are you all safe, is everyone there?" "We're alright up here," her daughter shouted back tearfully, "but we don't know what's happened downstairs to Emily and Frank. We heard a scream and we tried to get down the stairs to them, Mamma, but there was water coming up and we couldn't get past."

Her joy had now turned to horror on hearing that the two children from downstairs were not with them. Picking her way through the debris she pushed her way into the house, expecting to find the bodies of the two children in the mud on the floor. Casting her eyes frantically around the dark room she couldn't see any sign of the children until, looking up, she spotted the two still, naked bodies huddled together on the top shelf of the cupboard in the corner. She let out a horrified shriek, thinking that they were dead, and to her amazement, the children woke. Their mother lifted them down and as she tried to warm their shivering bodies they began to tell her about their frightening ordeal. "The bed was floating about and we thought we'd be thrown off into the water. We didn't know what was happening. We tried to get upstairs but it was blocked so we stood on the chair and climbed onto the shelf. What has happened Mamma? Where has all the water come from?" Mrs. Wells was unable to say. She had as little idea as they.

For other nearby families there was to be no such happy ending to the night. In nearby Cotton Mill Row, behind the Workhouse, one of the cottages was rented out, like so many in this poor part of town, in rooms, to a number of different families. Mrs. Wallace and her two children lived in a small downstairs room, partly below street level, so that when the water surged in they were in a desperate situation. Mrs Wallace managed to escape into the flooded yard screaming, "Help, someone help us. We'll all be drowned!" Above her a window was thrown open and a young man, seeing her danger, threw down a sheet. "Here, grab hold of this. Now hold on tightly." He pulled and the poor old woman was almost within his reach when an increased surge of water swept her off. There was a piercing scream and then no more as her body was flung away over the wall and she was lost to sight. Meanwhile, rescuers from the upper floor had reached the Wallace children and they were carried up to safety.

Only a few yards away, eighteen year old Sidney Varney was caught in the rising water whilst riding to his home in Kelham Street from his father's general store. The current was strong, but so was the horse and young Sidney may well have come through the night's adventure with nothing more than a wetting and an exciting story to tell for the rest of his life if a heavy piece of timber had not collided with the horse, causing it to stumble and throw its rider over its head. Both horse and rider struggled fiercely to regain a footing but the water was too deep and the force too strong and they too disappeared below the foaming black surface.

Right across the road outside The New Inn on Shalesmoor was deposited a huge piece of oak, carried by the flood from Butcher's works at Philadelphia, which must have weighed many tons. It was to present a spectacle for those travellers this way who were forced to negotiate the obstacle for weeks to come since it proved too heavy to move. Painters and photographers had plenty of time to record the amazing sight and there were many who were to pose sitting on it in their Sunday best for their first ever photograph. On the opposite side of the river the flood was now funnelled by the railway embankment towards the low lying area between Nursery Street and The Wicker, the closest that the flood would come to the town centre.

By the time that the flood had reached Lady's Bridge, word had already reached the ears of many of the people living in the crowded town centre courtyards and tenements that some excitement was afoot. Dozens now came rushing down Waingate, roused by passers by and neighbours hammering on doors as they passed, pulling on coats and hats, towards the ancient bridge to watch the spectacle. They were certainly not disappointed! A crowd of more than two hundred had soon huddled onto the bridge to experience the thrill of their lifetime as they leaned over the parapets and looked into the mass of dark water which foamed and raged against the arches. As more and more material was thrown up against the bridge the level of the water rose higher and higher until only those people in the centre were still on dry ground. The shaking of the structure added to the excitement, though, had they known that virtually every other bridge had been smashed that night they may have considered it more prudent to watch the fascinating spectacle from a safer distance! The whole experience had an exhilaration about it which made the young men on their precarious vantage point whoop and shout above the roar of the flood. Someone, leaning over to try to touch the water speeding below, spotted a rat clambering up the heap of debris to escape a watery end. "Knock him off!" came a cry, and some sport was had, as with calls and shouts, the young fellows ruthlessly dispatched the unfortunate creature.

Looking back towards the Wicker, however, rapidly caused the onlookers to pause and reconsider their own position. The scene was incredible. Water flowed everywhere. In the few remaining pools of light shed by the street lamps, scenes of carnage were glimpsed. Water flowed from every side street, bursting open the shuttered doors of the shops and pubs and carrying out a fantastic variety of merchandise. From the premises of Levi Fox, Number 74, flowed tin and wooden toys, artists materials and photographic equipment. From the drapers' shops were plucked the fashionable dresses, materials and dummies to ride the waves. John Walsh, the confectioner at Number 100, lost his stock of sweets; rifle balls, London mixtures, Prince Albert medals, bird's eyes, Nelson balls and ginger lozenges to name but a few. To the right, at Number 10 Blonk Street, the wave tore into the chemist and stationers shop of Joseph Hill Appleton, destroying his lending library stock of 3000 books and his entire stationary stock, amongst which was a large number of Valentines, unsold from February. A shout of horror went up as a naked man was picked out, clinging to a street lamp before being swept away before their eyes, and as other bodies and pathetic items of domestic furniture became apparent in the rushing tide the mood on the bridge became more sombre. Amidst it all the old bridge stood firm and survived its battering.

'The arches of Lady's Bridge were nearly choked by the accumulation of rubbish. The waters came rushing down with a force that made it quake and tremble.'

Samuel Harrison

* * * ** * * * * * * * *

Joseph Dyson, disturbed from his sleep in his house on Bond Street by repeated hammerings on the door, at last looked out. "What's happening? What's all the noise?" he called to someone hurrying by. "Oh, there's been an awful flood, and likely half of Sheffield drowned," came the reply. He made his way, following a steady stream of people, down Waingate. As he was passing the Town Hall, folks were coming up, ankle deep in mud. Across the river, near The Corner Pin, was a pile of mud a yard high. A filthy boy, his shirt sleeves rolled up, was reaching around in it, fishing out books. Dyson called the lad over and gave him a few coppers for a copy of Ovid's Poems. The inscription in the front cover showed it to have come from Damflask school. He tucked the book into his coat pocket and set off to explore the full course of the flood, and walked throughout the night, the full distance to Dale Dyke.

The shouting and hammering had been sufficient to warn most of the inhabitants of the network of tiny streets and lanes behind the Wicker of their impending peril. Most of them were safe from the deluge in upstairs rooms and so few were caught unawares. Seventeen year old Jonathan Turner, however, who lodged in a downstairs room in a cottage in Nursery Lane, was unprepared and suffered a fate as terrible as any that night. Imagine his terror to be woken by a great smashing noise and, starting up in alarm, to make out surging water bursting a hole through the corner of the room and pouring through it until his bed and furniture were swirling round in the torrent. The water rose higher and higher in the room and escape became impossible as the pressure held the door tight shut and so Jonathan could do nothing, but drowned in his own room as it filled to the ceiling with the freezing, black water. Now there came screams from a yard round the corner in Joiner Street as seventy-eight-year-old Dickie Hazlehurst was swept to his death from the box in which he slept in the shed of his coal yard, echoed by the screams of eleven pigs as they were similarly carried off or drowned as the water filled their sties. Through Lady's Bridge the flood swept round the sharp bend, scouring out the Killing Shambles and swirling Mr. Sneesby's sheep down the river, spilling over into the canal basin and setting the coal and steel barges moored there rocking and bobbing dangerously.

The pent-up flood now surged through the arches of the great railway viaduct, which carried the new Manchester line over the far end of The Wicker, and bore down on the Midland Railway Station, directly ahead. The double warehouse doors were stove in and the bodies of a man and a woman were carried in and swirled around the great shed. Engines stood marooned on the tracks and Richard Peacock, who worked for a coal dealer in the goods yard, and slept in an office on the premises, probably never woke as the rising water engulfed him.

But now the night's worst terrors were all but over for, although the dark flood spread over the lower Don Valley to cause immense damage to the vast new steelworks, invading the cellars, wrecking the crucible steel furnaces and ruining

67

the precious steel, the wave's terrible destructive power was spent. The viaduct had been the finishing gate of the wild, careering gallop, although the flood did have a final vindictive sting in its tail as both the nightwatchmen at Naylor's Vickers Steel Works and Hornby's Chemical works were overtaken in their flight from their flooded homes and were overcome by the rising tide. Thomas Gill was thus the flood's final tragic victim. The swollen river swept its burden of bodies and wreckage through Rotherham, Mexbrough and on towards Doncaster where, shortly after ten on the Saturday morning, there was still enough water to spill over the banks and flood the cellars of nearby homes and to deposit its grisly cargo and household treasures for the locals to pick over.

'Sad were the scenes which presented themselves, as groups of men, women and children, suddenly deprived of their homes, were to be seen wandering about in search of shelter and relief.'

The Aftermath

There was nothing more that John Gunson could usefully do at Dale Dyke. He had finally been persuaded to go back with Mr. Swinden to spend what remained of the night at his lodgings in Bradfield, but there had been no question of the engineer being able to sleep. At first light he had been back up to look closely at the wrecked dam wall. The scene was devastating. A huge untidy slice was missing from the centre of the embankment which had allowed the reservoir to all but completely empty. All that remained within the reservoir looked like a puddle in the middle of the huge expanse of wet mud. "I can't understand what's happened, Craven. The whole thing's collapsed, and yet we built it so carefully." "The embankment has given way above the point where the outlet pipes are buried. Do you think that could have had anything to do with it?" Gunson just shook his head. He was dog tired and in a state of shock. He knew now that it would be left for others to analyse whatever failings there had been. He turned and made his way towards the carriage to retrace his journey down the shattered valleys towards Sheffield.

* * * * * * * * * * * * *

The morning was breaking bright and clear on that dismal Saturday, revealing scenes of utter chaos along the Loxley and Don valleys. People who lived near the flooded area had slept little and daylight now revealed knots and groups of weary and dishevelled neighbours on every street corner, staring in disbelief, shaking their heads, unable to comprehend the cause of such a disaster. Many openly wept at the loss of family or friends. Women comforted grieving sufferers. Men pointed to some particularly striking feature or other and discussed the terrible force of the flood whilst children poked sticks into the sticky mud to retrieve bits and pieces which had been carried down. Lakes of stinking water still stood where the river had overflowed into low lying areas, and many people were stranded in homes which were still awash or surrounded by a sea of mud. None of them was aware of what had happened outside their own small locality and few in the town yet had any conception of the full scale of the disaster. The newspapers, however, had wasted no time in collecting first reports of the destruction. Newsboys were mobbed by news hungry crowds as soon as they emerged from the offices of *The Telegraph* and *The Independent*, where the presses had been rolling throughout the night. The whole edition of 54,000 copies could have been sold six times over. The population of Sheffield was stunned and normal life was suspended. Many of the factories in the Don Valley were closed, and some would remain so for weeks to come. Many workmen were idle, many had lost the tools of their trade and many families had lost their only breadwinner. With the pale daylight an awareness of the scale of the disastrous night's events gradually dawned on the bemused town.

It was still early when the chief constable, Mr. John Jackson, who had been busy directing operations since the early hours, sent for the Mayor, Thomas Jessop.

Together the two rode down to the Wicker and along Nursery Street. Jessop was particularly appalled by the scenes of terrible destruction. "I just couldn't have imagined that anything like this was possible, Mr. Jackson. Look at the gaslamps. They have been bent over with the force of the flood." "No, you have to see it to appreciate the full scale of the damage I think. Look, there are some of my men. It looks as if they've found another body."

The two men approached the front of The Manchester Railway Hotel. From a ragged hole torn through the front of the building a small group of policemen and helpers were emerging carrying the limp, muddy form of a girl. They carefully laid the body onto the back of a cart, to join several others which had already been collected. The Mayor removed his hat as the cart was led away towards the Workhouse, where many of the bodies were being laid, awaiting identification. Here the human cost of the night's proceedings was already being counted as Mr. Wescoe directed the parties of police and helpers to the straw covered rooms which were being set aside for this grim purpose. He could not know that within the next few days no less than one hundred and eighteen bodies, men and women, boys, girls and babies would be brought in. All along the route of the flood similar scenes were re-enacted as bodies were pulled from the mud or uncovered from piles of debris and taken to the nearest public house, school or police station.

Returning to the nearby Town Hall, just up the hill from Lady's Bridge, Thomas Jessop wasted no time in getting together with the Town Clerk, John Yeomans, and the coroner, John Webster. "Good morning Mr. Jessop, the news here is shocking." said the Town Clerk, looking up from the paper, "Are things really as bad as The Telegraph is reporting?" "Worse, far worse. I have been out with the Chief Constable and some of the things that we've seen I thought were unimaginable." "How many do you think have been killed then?" asked the coroner. "It's impossible to say yet, but I'm sure that the figure must run into hundreds. The bodies are being taken to the Workhouse. I think you had better go and see how they are managing." "Yes, I'll go straight down there. I will need to organise the identification and open the inquest on some of the victims, though I think there will be little doubt as to how they met their death!" "Yes, you carry on. Now, Mr. Yeomans, there is a great deal to be done. Firstly we must do all that we can to prevent the spread of disease. There are carcasses of dead animals all over. We will need quicklime, and plenty of it as quickly as possible." "I can arrange that, Mr. Jessop. We have received word that people have begun to loot the damaged houses in Hillsborough." "Good God, at a time like this. To think that people will steal from their own unfortunate neighbours! Well, we can put a stop to that. Have word sent to the barracks to ask the colonel if he will post infantrymen to stand guard." "I'll do that straight away. There are people outside who were caught up in the flood and have lost all their possessions. They are cold and wet, what shall I tell them to do?" "Well, I suppose that they can come into the Town Hall for the present. At least they can warm themselves by the fire. The overseers will arrange for the needs of all those who are destitute. We will arrange a meeting on Monday of the Council and prominent townspeople to begin to collect contributions for the relief of the suffering of the poor souls who have lost everything. Can you organise that? And, yes, you had better write to the Home Secretary to let him know what has happened here." "Certainly, I will get on with these things right away."

* * * * * * * * * * * * *

The detachment of soldiers which marched up from the Hillsborough barracks to the ruined village of Malin Bridge later in the day were far from the first on the scene. Already dozens of people had made their way there from the surrounding area to marvel and count their blessings. Only the soldiers who had seen active service overseas had experienced anything like this before, for the settlement appeared to have come under sustained heavy cannon bombardment. As in the aftermath of a battle bemused groups of homeless victims stood in huddles or sat hunched around cheerless campfires.

The ruins of The Cleakum Inn were especially striking, for the central chimney stack still stood with ragged remnants of the floors hanging from it. From this building George and Sarah Bisby and five of their children had been plucked to their deaths. Seventeen year old Mary, who had been away for the night, had hurried home to find what had become of her family. She stood now, sobbing and weeping, in front of the wrecked building, the only surviving member of the family. Frantically she searched here and there amongst the mud and ruins to salvage what pathetic bits and pieces she could, but there was precious little left. Concerned neighbours tried to console her terrible distress as best they could, by helping her to retrieve items and to offer her a few shillings. There was no sign of the bodies of her family for they, like most of the hundred people lost here, had been washed far down the river. Mary was to identify the bodies of her father and fourteen year old sister Tessa in the Workhouse the following Wednesday. Those of her mother, brothers and sisters were never to be identified.

The Town Clerk was busy in his office at the Town Hall, writing letters. First he wrote informing the Home Secretary of the disaster and asking that a Government Inspector be sent as quickly as possible to investigate the cause of the failure at Dale Dyke. Next he composed notices to appear in the newspapers asking that information on bodies discovered should be given to the police and that all property recovered should be handed in. He then set about writing to the great and good of the town inviting them to attend a special meeting on Monday afternoon to organise relief measures for the sufferers. John Webster was engaged in the melancholy task of receiving the bodies at the Workhouse, where he opened the inquest the same afternoon. Henry Pawson, the publisher, was elected foreman of the jury. The prospect of holding inquiries into the deaths of so many victims was daunting. "Could you ever have imagined anything like this, Mr. Pawson? Look at all these poor souls. I can't believe that the Water Company could be responsible for causing such terrible suffering. Someone will have to pay!" "How on earth can we possibly hold separate inquests on all these people?" said Pawson, "It could take weeks, and we don't yet know how many there will be in total." "We can't. You have seen the state that some of the corpses are in already," replied Webster. "We can't leave them unburied for more than a day or so. The risk to public health would be too great." "Then what are we to do?" "Well it must be clear to us all that these people have all met their death in the same circumstances. Don't you agree?" "Yes, there can be no doubt of that." "Then I suggest that we hold inquests on just a few, say three or four, and make these represent all the victims." "Yes, that sounds a reasonable way to proceed." "I will write to the Home Secretary to inform him of our intention and ask if this is acceptable. Which shall we choose for the inquest?" "I don't suppose it matters much. There are several here that have already been identified." Looking down the list which the overseer was still in the process of compiling, the names of Thomas Elston and his wife Elizabeth, from Neepsend lane, Keziah Eaton, who died following her husband in his vain attempt to save the pig, and Henry Fairhurst, a steel roller who died on the night shift at the Philadelphia Steel Works, were selected as the representatives of the victims.

As soon as the Town Clerk and the remaining jurors arrived Mr. Webster wasted no time in opening the inquest. "Gentlemen, once we have agreed a formal identification of a few of the bodies, I propose that the inquest be adjourned so that the Chief Constable and myself may have time to investigate some aspects of the failure of the dam wall. I will also be asking the Secretary of State's representative if the work was not examined and declared safe only several weeks ago. We will need to carefully investigate the rumour that the reservoir was known to be in a dangerous state on Friday and if so why no warning was issued. We must decide whether anyone was criminally liable or not." "Then I think we should take evidence from anyone who knew anything about the state of the dam on Friday", said William Woodhead. "I have spoken to a man called Ibbotson who told me that he had actually seen a crack and had been expecting a burst on Thursday," replied Joseph Walker. "He said that he had told the contractors about it but they had told him that it was perfectly safe." "I suggest that we all go to the site of the collapse as soon as possible, with an engineer, to familiarise ourselves with the details of the construction," said Webster and, this having been arranged for the following Monday, the inquest was adjourned until 23rd March. John Webster was so sure of the correctness of this procedure that, before informing the Home Secretary, he published notices to invite relatives to arrange for the burial of family members without the delay of an inquest. Fortunately for Webster the Home Secretary was in agreement.

'The number of visitors to the scene was perfectly enormous.'

The greeting which Webster gave to John Gunson as they met at The King's Head on the following Monday morning was as cold as the weather. For Gunson, looking hollow-eyed and drawn, the visit to Dale Dyke to accompany the coroner and jurymen was a continuation of the weekend's nightmare. To prolong the agony the horse-drawn omnibus, unable to negotiate the broken roads and bridges up the Loxley Valley, was forced to take the longer route, and pulled out of Sheffield on the Manchester Road, climbed the Rivelin Valley and crossed the bleak, high moorland at Strines. "Stop here please!" shouted Webster to the driver as they reached the ancient Strines farmhouse. From the head of the Loxley Valley here, the jury, now climbing down from the vehicle and, stretching their cramped legs, had a quite breathtaking view. The panorama of the valley with its villages, fields and farms was laid out before them. The great scar of the smashed embankment stretched across the scene below and, behind it, acres of gleaming mud clearly outlined the former extent of the reservoir, now virtually empty. "Looking from here it is easy to see why the reservoir was planned for this position, I think" said Webster, directing his remarks towards the engineer. "Yes, over forty inches of rain falls on the moors here so we could be sure of a constant supply of water to maintain the level in the reservoir." "How much water was it designed to hold when full?" "About 700,000,000 gallons," replied John Gunson. "It was unfortunate that the dam wall was not strong enough to hold it then," remarked Webster in an undertone as he turned to climb back on the bus.

As the bus trundled down the valley towards the construction site the jury found that they were far from the only visitors to Dale Dyke. They pulled up beside dozens of carriages and carts, all hired out by the more enterprising citizens of Hillsborough, who were doing brisk trade transporting the hoards of visitors along the course of the flood. Many of the sightseers had travelled from far afield, taking advantage of the 'Excursion Specials' put on by the railway companies and were being given tours by self-appointed guides. Ladies in crinolines, children in sailor suits and men in tall hats and capes, all expressed opinions on the cause of the collapse although few, of course, had any real knowledge of civil engineering. Most were awestruck by the tremendous scale of the work, and the newspaper reports struggled to find meaningful comparisons of its size. The Illustrated London News, for example, helpfully suggested that their readers might be able to visualise the tremendous volume of water which had been released down the valley by imagining the whole 113,000,000 cubic feet filling a cistern large enough to contain St. Pauls Cathedral, the cross of which would still be fifty feet under water!

All in all the spectacle had the ingredients of a fine day out, and over 150,000 people took advantage of the opportunity in the first few days, running the gauntlet of the hawkers, cheats and vagabonds who were also making the most of their opportunity. Amongst them there were frauds, claiming to be destitute as a result of the flood, who boasted of earning more than twelve pounds a day by begging, the equivalent of three months pay for a working man. Where there were crowds there were thieves and John Jackson's overstretched police force was inundated with complaints from their victims. Alderman Gledrill, who had come from Salford, and Mr. Hughes from Manchester complained that, whilst stretching to get a view through the window of the bodies of victims who had been brought to lay in Hillsborough National School, they had had their watches stolen from their pockets. The gold watch belonging to Charles Price, the storekeeper at Malin Bridge, was, however, recovered from the mud by someone who had the good grace to return it to his relatives. One particular personal remnant from Malin Bridge which came into the possession of others, however, never found its way back. George Froggatt of Rawmarsh pulled from the swollen river beyond Rotherham a beautifully embroidered sampler. It was exquisitely worked with a complicated design featuring flowers, trees, exotic birds and a house, in front of which was a pond with ducks and geese. The name 'Anne Tricket, 1815' had been carefully stitched at the bottom. George Froggatt who carefully reframed the embroidery and hung it on the wall of the kitchen, knew nothing of the family to whom it had so recently belonged.

As well as visiting the highlights of the tour, which included such 'picturesque' ruins as The Cleakum Inn and Brick Row, the visitors were excited to see that, by hiring one of the photographers using the new photographic techniques, they could record their visit for posterity. If they could not afford that, at least they could buy a postcard with a photographic print for their friends to marvel at when they got home, making this the first major disaster to be comprehensively recorded in photographs.

Members of the inquest jury picked their way along the embankment until they came to the untidy gash which the water had sliced through it. Webster wasted no time in voicing the thoughts of the men as they looked into the gap. "This material seems to me to be little more than loose rubble, Mr.Gunson. Can you explain to us how the dam wall was constructed?" "The embankment was built in the usual way, although the puddle trench had to be built much deeper than we originally intended because of all the water that we encountered. In the end it was sixty feet deep. "How did you make the wall watertight then?" asked Henry Pearce. "We had to keep pumping it out continually for two years and then we filled the trench with best puddled clay which would be quite impervious." "Then what happened to the water which had been flowing into the trench?" "The springs would simply be stopped by the clay and the water would come up into the reservoir. We then proceeded to build up the puddle wall with carefully graded material on either side to support it to the full height." "And where are the outlet pipes?" "They are now buried deep in the embankment near where we are standing. They were laid diagonally through the puddle wall," replied Mr. Gunson. "Then how could they be checked for leakage?" retorted the coroner. "They were carefully laid and tested. There should be no reason to think that they could leak." But John Webster was, not for the last time, growing impatient with what he perceived as evasive answers. "I do not see how you can say that. There seems to have been too much left to chance. The possibility of water creeping along these pipes and weakening the wall must have occurred to you! And what if one had fractured? Surely that is a possibility considering the vast weight laid on top of them." "I can only repeat that everything was done to the highest specifications. The pipes were fitted together in six inch sockets and these were sealed with lead. I do not think there could have been any leakage. I never saw water seeping through the embankment and until it burst I never saw anything to cause concern." "Then what do you think caused it to collapse?" Gunson shook his head. "I do not know."

There were many self-appointed experts, however, who were only too ready to offer their own explanations for the disaster, and most of these were clear that the blame lay in the design and construction techniques of the dam. The feature that most people were having difficulty understanding was that the massive construction did not rely on any stonework for its stability or water-holding capacity. Many expressed disbelief that the builders could have put their faith in what, they saw for themselves, was little more than an unconsolidated mass of loose rubble. As today, the press compounded these fallacies.

'On Monday, March 14th, the Coroner and the Jury proceeded to examine the reservoir.'

The observations of the local people, however, must deserve attention. After all, they had farmed the fields stretching up the valley sides for generations. They knew every lie of the land and their walls were built from the local sandstones. Their reflections indicate that some of them had long held reservations about the construction site chosen for the huge wall. It was Joseph Ibbotson, the miller from Bradfield, who expressed the opinions of the whole community in writing a letter to *The Sheffield Telegraph*, and there were few better qualified than he to do so. After all, he and his brothers had been present when the first sods were turned, over five years ago, and had later stood in that great trench before it was filled. They had watched with some foreboding as the great embankment steadily rose, month by month, and, had they been entirely satisfied by the contractors' reassurances, the whole family would have been wiped out when it failed. "What I think we should start with," said Richard Ibbotson, " is about how the place where the dam is built has always been liable to landslips." "Aye, that's right enough. You remember they had to move a little way further up from where they were first going to build it because the rocks were all broken up," replied Joseph. "And then I think we should mention the springs that we saw pouring out from the bottom of the puddle trench right up to the time that we filled it with clay. I think that water must have been coming from inside the reservoir itself. I know that the clay stopped it flowing but just imagine the immense pressure it must have put on the clay wall when the eighty feet of water in the dam was added to the sixty foot depth." "I'm sure you're right. The springs were right in the place where it collapsed. And, of course, don't forget that the part of the embankment that collapsed was the last to be built, since we started at both ends and worked towards the middle. It stands to sense that the parts of the bank nearest the ends got packed down more tightly as we rolled over them with the carts and trucks." "Yes, but I think you were closer to the truth of the matter when you were talking about the landslips," replied Richard. "On Saturday when I went up to Dale Dyke I saw an opening in the ground running from the bank to the farmhouse. I was told that it runs right through the house and that one part of the stone floor has sunk." The miller nodded. "Yes. It must be clear to anyone that even the best formed embankment can only be as firm as its foundations."

* * * * * * * * * * * * *

At Roebuck House, one of the first farmsteads in the valley to feel the flood's impact, twenty three year old Selina Marsden and her husband were just returning after a harrowing ordeal. They had responded to the notices posted by John Webster for persons to assist in the grim work of identifying the bodies. They had felt it their duty to go straight down to Malin Bridge where many of the victims had been brought to the school. Many years later, as an old lady, Selina was to remember this occasion as vividly as she did the terror of the flood itself. In an interview for an article in The Independent she recalled, 'The bodies were all laid on benches and looked like beautiful waxworks. They lay side by side, an aged man beside a little child, perhaps his grandson. In other cases husband and wife lay together, and in some instances, whole families. When I saw the sight I turned to my husband and we gave thanks to God for our providential escape.' The elderly lady still owned her precious Bible, one of the many which bore the inscription

'A Gift of The British and Foreign Bible Society,
to Replace The Bible Lost in The Sheffield Flood
During the Night of 11 March, 1864.'

The grim search for the remains of missing relatives and friends continued apace and Monday's newspapers bore columns of poignant personal advertisements such as the following;

LOST IN THE FLOOD

From Hillfoot Bridge, a man about 33 years, bald with thin light whiskers round the face; height about five foot five inches and with a scar on his right thigh caused by an abscess being cut. Information will be gratefully received by Charles Pickering, Red lion Inn, Trippett Lane, Sheffield.

Meanwhile the coroner had been busy collating the information which was coming in from all along the course of the flood and making it available to the newspapers as quickly as possible. The following appeared on the 12th.

TO THE PUBLIC, It is requested that the following bodies may be IDENTIFIED if possible before noon on Tuesday next, after which time the police will direct their interment;
A man, unknown, lying at The Plumpers Inn, Tinsley, about 42 years of age.
A man, unknown, Lying at Joseph Taylor's, Don Close, Greasbro, about 25 years of age.
A man and girl, unknown, at The Holmes Tavern, Kimberworth, man about 40, girl about 10 years of age.
Two women, unknown, at The Angel Inn, Rotherham, one about 50, the other about 40 years of age.
One man, one boy and three women, unknown, lying at The Ship Inn, Kilnhurst, man about 45, boy 16, and women 40, 28 and 47.
A man, from 45 to 50. A woman about 45 and a child about 3 at The Montagu Arms, Mexbro.
J. Webster, Coroner, Sheffield, March 12th, 1864.

Distraught relatives scanned the stark descriptions, looking for clues from which they might identify their loved ones. The descriptions, however were vague and many unfortunate people had the added distress of touring round many public houses and schools, scrutinising dozens of bodies before finding the ones they were searching for, if they ever did. John Appleby from Hillsborough, for example, made trips to Kilnhurst, Wath, Mexbrough and Doncaster before locating the body of his wife, Mary, in Rotherham.

*   *   *   *   *   *   *   *   *   *   *   *   *

While Webster and the jury were inspecting the site of the fractured dam wall the Mayor was presiding over the hastily arranged meeting of the town's most prominent citizens in the council chamber of the Town Hall. It was an interesting party comprising not politicians, statesmen, artists, writers or great landowners but

As soon as news of the calamity reached Mr. Jackson, the Chief Constable, he mounted his horse and rode into the inundated districts, at great personal risk, to render assistance. Here he is seen directing operations at Philadelphia.

steelmakers, cutlers and silversmiths, the great entrepreneurs of nineteenth century Sheffield. John Brown, of The Atlas Steel Works, Mark Firth, from The Norfolk Works, and Edward Vickers of the River Don Works, George Wostenholm, from the immense Washington cutlery works and the silversmiths, James Dixon and Frederick Mappin were amongst those who had responded so promptly to Thomas Jessop's invitation. "Gentlemen, I have called this meeting so that we may consider what measures might be adopted to alleviate the sufferings caused by this terrible flood. I think that by now we are all only too well aware of what has happened. I would like to suggest that a Public Meeting be held here tomorrow in order to establish a relief fund for the sufferers." There was general agreement to this proposal and Mr. Dunn moved a resolution to this effect. "All those who have travelled up the valley will be aware of the vast amount of distress which has been caused, not just the mental distress brought about from the loss of family or friends, but real bodily suffering from loss of property and want of food and clothing." John Brown seconded the motion in his typical, blunt style. "I feel persuaded that, as Sheffield men, we shall deal with this matter in a practical manner. We have before us substantial marks of wreck, distress and loss of life, and our first duty and desire will be, as in times past, to meet and relieve, in a practical and warm hearted manner, the sad consequences now before us, without stopping to investigate the cause of the calamity or who is to blame for it. Let us put our names down for something at once, and not let that which is already bad be made worse by delay." Lord Wharncliffe, from Wortley Hall, who had entered the chamber whilst John Brown was speaking, was quick to take up the same theme, betraying, as he spoke, strong elements of the traditional Sheffield inferiority complex. "About a year ago I addressed you in this hall on the distress in Manchester and we contributed, I may say, handsomely. But now our feelings must be warmer and more sincere as our fellow townsmen and neighbours need assistance. We must lay aside every thought of niggardliness and avarice, and come down handsomely for the credit of the town. The town of Sheffield has not occupied the position in the eyes of England in this particular as it ought to have done. I don't think we are held in equal estimation with some towns of smaller populations and less prosperous trade, but events like this, which call us together, give us opportunities to raise ourselves in this matter. Don't pinch your contributions!"

Even as he spoke hands were reaching deep into ample pockets all round the room and pledges of money were quickly forthcoming, £200 from the Mayor, and a similar amount from John Brown, James Dixon, Vickers, Firths, Sandersons and others, until the total amount subscribed from the meeting had reached a splendid £4,775.

* * * * * * * * * * * * *

It was late on that busy Monday night that the Mayor could be found with a party of town hall officials on the platform of the Midland Station, just beyond the Wicker Arches. None of the usual ceremony that would accompany the greeting of a government official was apparent. An engine steamed into the station and Mr.

Robert Rawlinson, the Inspector sent by the Home Secretary to investigate the cause of the failure of the embankment, stepped down onto the still muddy platform. His self-assured air came from long experience in his field of civil engineering. This was not the first time that the Government had turned to him following upheavals in various parts of the country and abroad. The effects of the deluge were already plain for him to see and to smell. Thomas Jessop stepped forward. "Mr. Rawlinson? We are pleased to welcome you to Sheffield, but sorry that your journey should have been made necessary by such a terrible event." "Thank you. I hope that I may be of some assistance to you. It would seem that this was part of the town which was affected by the flood." "Yes. Much urgent work has been done already, but there is still a great deal of work to do to clear away the mud and debris and to help those that have lost everything." "I'm sure that you are doing all that you can in such difficult circumstances." "You will be tired after your long journey," replied the Mayor. "We have booked a room for you here at The Royal Victoria Hotel. I trust that you will have all that you need there." "Yes, I think that I will sign in straight away and then make an early start and take a look at the dam itself in the morning." After walking across the road and up the steps beside the imposing railway arches above The Wicker the inspector bid the group goodnight and booked into his room at The Station Hotel.

Early the following morning of Tuesday 15th March, Mr. Rawlinson met with the Mayor, the Town Clerk and the Coroner at the Town Hall in order to bring himself up to date with the details of the disaster and the relief of the victims, before setting off with John Webster up to Dale Dyke to investigate for himself. It was a remarkable journey, and one which Rawlinson would never forget. The gig followed the low road up the Don Valley beyond Shalesmoor so that the Coroner could give Mr. Rawlinson an impression of the scale of the devastation. It was not difficult to grasp. All along the valley were wrecked houses, great piles of timber, broken furniture and machinery jutting out at ugly angles. A layer of filthy wet mud still coated most of the streets and the height of the flood could easily be gauged from the muddy tidemarks half way up many of the damaged houses. Cleaning up operations were evident everywhere as people attempted to sweep the filth from their homes into the clogged drains. To the right Webster pointed out the ruins of Waterloo Houses, a row of about eight cottages next to Cornish Works. They presented an extraordinary sight as the flood water had stripped away the front wall from the whole row leaving the interiors exposed to view like an enormous open air stage set. Canaries still trilled from their cages, which hung from bare walls and workmen were busy erecting boarding to prevent any more of the contents from being taken. Not that there was much left, most of it having been washed out during the flood. The Government Inspector was appalled. "I knew that the flood had caused a great deal of damage," he said, "but I had no idea that it was as extensive as this. When I am satisfied that I have gathered as much evidence as I need at Dale Dyke I think I had better investigate the extent of the destruction caused, to put in my report to the Home Secretary. It is beginning to seem that I will need someone else from London to help me."

They carried on towards Hillsborough where the bridge, fortunately, was not entirely destroyed, and up the Loxley. On their left the ruins of Brick Row had

The gravestones of (clockwise) the Trickets, in Bradfield Churchyard, John Bower and the Armitages, outside Loxley Chapel, and the Price family, at Wadsley.

attracted a crowd of sightseers. It looked as though huge jaws had taken a bite from the lower corner of the great brick block. Chairs, tables and beds still hung precariously on three legs on the remaining fragments of the first and second floors high above the street. As they came to the ruins of Malin Bridge the travellers were struck by the unexpected crowds of visitors. Had it not been for the terrible scene of devastation in front of them they might easily have mistaken the scene for a gala! The well-to-do in their finery and the working people were assailed by the cries of vendors of meat pies and drinks from wayside stalls as they trekked up and down the stricken valley. Self-styled artists and poets hawked cheap engravings of the most graphic ruins and long doggerel verses to the souvenir-hungry visitors at a penny a sheet. Rawlinson and Jackson considered it thoroughly unseemly.

It was late in the morning when they reached Dale Dyke. John Gunson was there to meet them. He had instructions from the Company to give the Inspector whatever assistance he required. For the next couple of hours the Inspector examined every aspect of the work, constantly questioning Mr. Gunson and making detailed notes and sketches about technical details of flow rates, capacity and dimensions which had been beyond the knowledge of the Coroner and the inquest jury on the previous day. At least John Gunson felt that he was now talking to a fellow engineer who understood the principles and complexities of a construction of this scale. At one point Rawlinson requested that a party of workmen be asked to clear an area inside the embankment so that he could examine the nature of the bare rock itself, which he did with a great deal of interest.

Back at the Royal Victoria Hotel, late that afternoon, Rawlinson sat down to write a report on the day's proceedings to Lord Grey. It soon became clear that he had already formed strong opinions about the cause of the disaster and was not reticent about expressing them at such an early stage. He was critical of the fact that much of the material to build the bank had been taken from the bed of the reservoir. "The engineers have allowed the sandstone rock to be stripped bare," he wrote, "and I have seen that this is cracked and jointed. There can be little doubt that this would have allowed water to leak under pressure. It would seem that the outlet pipes were too small and laid in a quite improper manner and that the bywash weir was incorrectly constructed. Although I have not been able to examine the puddle wall, it is clear that the embankment has been built far too loosely. I enclose a sketch map that I made at the site. I would suggest that this information should go no further at present as I have been asked by the Coroner to give my views as evidence to the Inquest as well as to act as the expert witness on behalf of the jury. I do not altogether think that this is a proper way to proceed and I would welcome legal opinion on this."

* * * * * * * * * * * * *

The first of the burials took place on the Tuesday. The Poor Law Guardians made coffins available to those poor families who could not afford them and buried those without surviving families. There was no public ceremony and no mass burial, in fact in many cases there was no one left to mourn. Twelve Armitages were buried side by side in a plot behind Loxley Chapel. The Trickets found a resting place beside the bodies of their infants in the windswept graveyard at Bradfield, the Prices were laid to rest in the shadow of Wadsley Church and the Alberts joined the serried rows of paupers graves in the lower section of the General Cemetery. Despite the monumental scale of the disaster no monument was erected to the victims of the flood, although a handful of gravestones provide us today with an altogether more poignant reminder of that tragic night. The lines carved on them speak of a terrible acceptance of the vengeful actions of an unpredictable God. On the Trickets' headstone is carved;

> *Whoever may be blamed for our recent distress,*
> *Our duty to God it makes none the less.*
> *Whate'er be the fault, these words are true,*
> *The flood is a warning to me and to you.*

Most people today, I think, would consider this somewhat censorious considering that eleven of the Tricket household had been swept to their deaths. The inscription on the Armitages' huge rounded headstone reiterates the theme, and continues to draw a heavy-handed moral from the family's fate;

> *The evil that besets our path*
> *Who can prevent or cure.*
> *We stand upon the brink of death*
> *When most we seem secure.*
>
> *If we today sweet peace possess*
> *It soon may be withdrawn,*
> *Some change may plunge us in distress*
> *Before to morrows dawn.*

It was to be almost two months later, when the body of nine year old Jonathan Ibbotson was identified on May 5th, that the last of the dead could finally be laid to rest, although even then there were some twenty individuals who were still not accounted for.

* * * * * * * * * * * *

In the packed chamber of the Town Hall, at 2 o'clock sharp, the Mayor stood to bring to order the meeting which had been convened the previous day. It was a few moments before Mr. Jessop could quieten the excited and noisy throng, amongst whom the town's prominent tradespeople were well represented, so that he could introduce the first speaker, Earl Fitzwilliam, who was greeted with loud cheering. "This fearful inundation, which has caused such immense destruction of property and such widespread misery and desolation calls upon the inhabitants of this Borough at once to subscribe to a fund to alleviate the great distress," he began.

"Our first priority must be to assist those who have lost everything and, in particular, those families who have suffered the loss of the breadwinner. I am pleased to report that large sums have already been pledged and my family and I wish to donate £1000. I trust that the Mayor and his committee will use it quickly to benefit those who most need it." Loud cheering and applause punctuated the Earl's speech and this continued as Lord Wharncliffe rose to his feet. "The Mayor informs me that the sum of £6,000 has already been subscribed. Although this is one of those calamities which no human means can totally alleviate, the example has been set by the highest in this room and I think that it should be followed down to the lowest. I hope that we shall find the whole of England will rally to render assistance to us in this hour of need, but we must first set our own shoulders to the wheel. We must set the example!" Loud cheering again broke out and it was clear that the resolution found favour with the several hundred men in the crowded room. Thomas Jessop rose again, "I wish to express our thanks for your support. There can be no doubt that all those present today will follow your most generous example and rise to the challenge before us and that the committee appointed to collect and distribute the donations will do so as promptly and efficiently as they are able. Is there anyone who wishes to speak?" Mr. James Dodworth, a cutlery manufacturer, was the first to catch the Mayor's eye. "I have been speaking to my men and we are of the opinion that the working men of the town should give up one day's pay for the relief fund. In this way £10,000 could be easily raised." "I know that the working men of Sheffield are open hearted and ever ready to assist their fellow workmen in distress," replied the Mayor, "And I know how the poor can help the poor. I think that there are few men who would feel it a hardship to do this." "Should the men who have had their houses flooded be expected to contribute to their factories?" came a shout from the crowd which struck a discordant note. The comment was met with derisive laughter and jeers. "No man would be expected to give more than he could afford," retorted the Mayor, turning to the next speaker, Mr. Henry Levy, who kept a shop in the High Street. "I have placed a box outside my shop in which passers-by could place pennies for the fund. I have here 2,894 pennies here which I will leave with the treasurer." "Thank you Mr. Levy. Now, Mr. Sales." "I think that the people of Sheffield have done their duty most nobly. We must all help in our own way. I am pleased to announce that my warehouse on Pepper Alley will be open to receive old clothing and from there it will be distributed to the distressed."

The subscriptions flooded in, not only from the manufacturers and working people of Sheffield, but from virtually every town in England, and later in the week the Relief Committee felt honoured to receive a letter from the Queen containing her commiserations and a cheque for £200. The General Committee of the Bradfield Inundation Relief Fund, as it was long-windedly titled, worked tirelessly and in the next two months the sum of £50,000 had been collected. Donations were made to all those who presented themselves with evidence of their need so that by the end of April over 20,000 people had received help from the committee with donations of food, clothing or furniture. Volunteers from the committee visited the devastated homes in the affected areas, proffering what help they could. Vast numbers of pairs of shoes, having been left downstairs, were lost. The committee replaced 4,407 pairs. Another pressing need was to replace the tools of working men lost in the flood. £1,333 was spent on providing replacements. At the beginning of May it became apparent that enough money had been collected to relieve the cases of urgent distress and notices were issued to the effect that further donations would not be required. Public generosity and the goodwill of the townspeople had been asked to respond to the disastrous events and they had done so handsomely. The immediate needs had been met. Now it was left for the Water Company and the coroner to battle over culpability and compensation.

* * * * * * * * * * * *

At the Eagle Works on Mowbray Street, Sarah Jane Green was counting her blessings as she finally got down to writing the much delayed letter to her grandmother in Leeds. "I have no doubt that you will be most anxious to hear how we have got on," she wrote. "Aunt was woken by the screaming of pigs, and when she got up and lifted the blind, she saw the water rolling wave over wave. She woke uncle and I, and uncle went downstairs to look. The water had risen three steps, and, just as he told us, the gas went out and we had only half a candle. Aunt and I gave ourselves up for lost and uncle said that if it should come up any higher we should have to get on the roof. However, when he went down again, he found the water lower. Oh, how thankful we were to hear that! We went back to bed but we could not sleep. In the morning we had no fire, no bread nor anything, and the worst of it was, our kitchen was four or five inches in mud. Almost all the furniture is spoiled, the piano is smashed, and almost all the household things are ruined, but aunt says she cannot murmur because there are so many poor souls so much worse off than we. One poor family opposite us had nothing to eat nor a bit of fire until about four o'clock on Saturday afternoon. You may be sure we are all of us very grateful. I remain you affectionate granddaughter, S.J.G."

Relics of the Flood

SIMPLE WOODEN CHAIR.

A SMALL BIBLE

Kelham Island Museum

The Reckoning

In the immediate aftermath of the disaster the Water Company kept an understandably low profile and it wasn't until March 21st that the company chairman, William Smith, issued a statement to the concerned shareholders. Not surprisingly the value of the shares had fallen dramatically following the disaster, to a quarter of their previous price, and the investors were frightened that, if the Company's funds were insufficient to cover the claims against it, they would be personally liable. Mr. Smith wrote reassuringly that, whilst the Company felt great regret over the tragic events, they were actively seeking the best legal representation with regard to the company's liability. It is easy to understand why the directors should be so uneasy about their legal position. The company had been incorporated in 1853, the year following the Holmfirth flood, and so strict penalties had been introduced to cover just such contingencies. Not that anyone at the time ever considered that these would come into effect, but the Act required the Company to;

'Pay for and make good to the owners of all mills, buildings highways, bridges and manufactories and every injured person whatsoever, all loss, costs, damages and expenses incurred through the failure of the reservoir or embankment,'

which must be as clear and straightforward a statement of the Company's position as could be imagined. Legal advisors were of the same opinion, although they did express the view that, whilst the Company was clearly responsible for the cost of claims for damage and injury, this liability should not extend to the private property of the shareholders. The ruling was met with some relief, and not only by the shareholders themselves, for, whilst the Water Company understandably came in for a great deal of criticism, there were also those who expressed sympathy for its plight.

* * * * * * * * * * * * *

Few people showed such sentiments at the inquest, which resumed at ten o'clock on the morning of Wednesday, 23rd March in the Town Hall, when the Coroner, John Webster, was to betray personal antagonisms against the Company quite inappropriate to his position. The inquest had drawn together all the major characters in this drama under one roof, to play out its final act. Samuel Hammerton, the farmer who had first noticed the crack, sat with the Ibbotsons. Thomas Jessop and other members of the Town Council were acknowledged with a nod by The Chief Constable, John Jackson, as they took their seats. William Smith was huddled in urgent deliberations with the other directors of the Water Company, but already seated were the elegantly dressed John Towlerton Leather and the hunched figure of John Gunson, the engineers. Beside them sat the lawyers engaged to represent the Company, Mr. Perronet Thompson and Mr. Blakelock Smith. Behind them sat the contractors, Craven and Fountain. To the side of the room the reporters, William Leng and Samuel Harrison already had their notebooks out, jotting down the name of each person as they entered. Last to enter, by a door at the front of the courtroom, were the government engineers, Robert Rawlinson and Nathaniel Beardmore closely followed by John Webster, the Coroner.

The court went quiet as the last few people took their seats, the murmurings died down and Webster prepared to address the jury to his left. Emotions in the courtroom were running high. The final death toll of two hundred and forty people had appalled people and they were eager to lay the responsibility at someone's door. John Gunson was well aware of the strength of feeling and it seemed to weigh heavily on him. Here should have been the opportunity to present and weigh the facts in a measured and deliberate manner to arrive at a carefully considered verdict. In the event the inquest was a clumsy and ill-tempered affair which did no credit to the town's reputation or the memory of those who had died. During the two days John Webster's hectoring and bullying manner frequently betrayed his own prejudices and cut short lines of questioning which could have proved informative, and at the end the verdict was thoroughly unsatisfactory.

"Although we are here to inquire into the circumstances of the deaths of Thomas Elston and others on March 12th we will, in fact, hear very little about these people," began the Coroner. "Instead I propose to examine all those with a knowledge of the construction of the embankment at Dale Dyke to establish the cause of this disaster." Indeed, Webster appeared to be setting himself up as a one man commission of inquiry and even with his opening remarks to be exceeding his brief. True to his word, the first witness that he called to give evidence was not one of the witnesses to the dam's collapse but Mr. Leather, its designer. "Please tell us who you are and then explain to us your part in the construction of the dam." "I am the consulting engineer of the Sheffield Water Works Company and as such I prepared the plans and specifications for the construction of the reservoir." John Towlerton Leather spoke clearly and commandingly as he continued at length to explain the process of sinking the puddle trench and the difficulties which had been encountered. "It was necessary to continue to sink the trench until a watertight foundation was reached, which we did when we reached a depth of sixty feet." "Did water continue to flood into these workings?" "Certainly, a great deal of water came into the trench during the working." "Then how did you get rid of it?" "We used steam pumps." "And did you inspect the work yourself?" "I came when I was wanted. I saw the trench, I think, twice, once in 1861 and again in 1863." "Do you know what happened to the water in the trench once it was filled with clay?" "Nothing would happen to it. It would simply be blocked off. That is the purpose of the puddle wall."

The engineer then went on to explain how the bank was built. "The stone, clay, shale and earth to build the bank was taken from the inside of the reservoir." "How was it built up?" "I cannot say. That was Mr. Gunson's responsibility. He was not my servant!" snapped Mr. Leather testily, irritated at being continually interrupted in his evidence by the coroner's interjections. "Two eighteen-inch pipes were laid from the inside of the reservoir underneath the embankment in a trench nine feet below the ground," continued Leather. "And what would be the consequence of the fracture of one of these pipes?" asked Webster. "It would be serious, I suppose. The embankment might collapse, but I can't tell. I never heard of anything like that happening." "Is it not common for the joints of new pipes to leak?" put in Rawlinson. "Ours were strenuously tested." "But my experience is that they can give way." "Well that is not my experience," replied Mr. Leather. "How quickly could you lower the level of water in the reservoir through these pipes?" asked Webster. "The pipes would run off about 10,000 cubic feet of water per minute, so it would take about nine days to empty the reservoir at this rate." "But don't you think that you ought to have had more control over the water?" "I had not thought so before, but such events as these can cause us to reconsider our views. Besides, great damage can be done by letting off too much water too quickly." "But not as much as letting it all off at once! You should have done all you could to minimise the danger here and there has been no attempt to do so." " Oh yes there has!" "No there has not. You have placed a great embankment there and collected an immense body of water behind it, but, even though there was a suspicion that the embankment might give way, you provided no means of taking the water in any other direction, so as to avoid it coming down in a body on the people of Sheffield!"

This might have been good, knockabout entertainment, providing excellent copy for the reporters who sat scribbling frantically, but it was clear that such emotive outbursts were not likely to lead to a carefully considered verdict. And this was only the first morning. "What is the cause of the embankment bursting?" asked the Coroner directly. "I really do not know." "You must have an opinion on it, everyone in the town does." An uncomfortable snigger ran round the courtroom. "I have no opinion which is worth much, but I believe that the rocks below the embankment may have slipped." "Then you do not ascribe the bursting of the reservoir to unsound principles of engineering or to bad workmanship?" "Certainly not!"

Mr. Leather could have hardly been expected to say anything else. He was now allowed to stand down and it was the turn of John Gunson to stand forward, and, having witnessed the little respect that Webster had shown for his superior, the resident engineer did so with considerable foreboding. However, by the time that Gunson had been speaking for a while, carefully and deliberately detailing the process of digging the trench and building the wall, both the jury and those attending had become impressed by his clear grasp of the principles and attention to detail. Here was a man of obvious integrity. Following this long delivery the engineer mentioned that the Agden reservoir, the second in the Bradfield scheme of reservoirs, was being built on the same principles. "I hope not!" interjected the coroner. "What if the pipes burst there? What will be the effect?" "The same as we have seen" replied Gunson, taken completely off guard. "You don't anticipate it will burst?" "No." "But I do! Suppose a pipe is fractured. How would you get to it?" "That would be difficult." "Do you not think that it would have been better to construct the dam in the first place so that you could get at the pipes?" "Yes, if we had assumed there could be a fracture, but we did not apprehend any danger." Turning to the jury for greater effect Webster commented "And that was the fault that Mr. Leather and the witness committed. Neither of them would look before them."

Not to be so lightly dismissed, John Gunson felt impelled to defend his unblemished record. "We have made eight reservoirs." "Then you have made eight mistakes!" retorted Webster, angrily. A buzz went round the courtroom. "Really, sir. I must object," put in Perronet Thompson, rising to his feet. "Such observations should not be made in the presence of the jury." "I am simply trying to get these engineers to speak like rational men. Everyone could see that the method of construction was dangerous and now two hundred and fifty Sheffielders are dead. You have only to visit the site to see that it was inevitable and now they are building another in the same way. There will be the same mischief." It took a little while for the court to settle again after this outburst, but Webster was quickly resuming his intimidation of Mr. Gunson. "Tell us what happened on the day of the flood. There is a rumour that you said during that day something about the embankment giving way." "I never said such a thing! I had gone home in the afternoon convinced that all was safe and never expected that it would burst."

The second day provided interludes no less dramatic than the first. The first witness to be called was Matthew Jackson, an eminent civil engineer with considerable experience of constructing reservoirs in Melbourne, Australia. After giving detailed evidence regarding the usual method of construction of such embankments, Jackson concluded that, in his opinion, the failure of the dam had been caused by water escaping into the bank from the outlet pipes which may have ruptured due to uneven pressure caused by the embankment settling or the joints being forced apart by the immense pressure of water inside them. "So we could shorten this inquiry if the Water Works Company would pay to have the pipes excavated," said Mr. Webster. Mr. Smith, for the Company, quickly rose to reply, "I cannot pledge the Company to anything without consideration. They wish, like the public, to do everything possible to ascertain the cause of this accident, but at present we are fighting in the dark. I must submit, the question for the jury is simply whether anyone is criminally responsible." "If you wish we can soon find Mr. Leather guilty of manslaughter and send this for further investigation to York," replied the Coroner. Mr. Leather shifted uncomfortably in his seat. "That, surely, is a matter for the jury, Mr. Webster," said Blakelock Smith.

Mr. Bland, one of the jurors, fortunately stepped in at this point to ask if there was any means by which the pipes could be examined. Robert Rawlinson replied that since there was such a violent disturbance of the ground when the embankment collapsed, even if a dozen fractures were found it could not be stated for certain that this occurred before the flood. This apparently promising line of inquiry had, therefore, to be little more than conjecture. Mr. Gunson was recalled at this point and Mr. Webster resumed the offensive. "Mr. Gunson, we have heard that you constructed the embankment to the specifications drawn up by Mr. Leather. Is that correct?" "Yes sir." "Did you deviate from these specifications at all", "Yes, we had to make allowance for particular circumstances," replied John Gunson. "Then what is the purpose of a specification if you are not going to keep to it?" "It is a guide." "Was Mr Leather aware that you were ignoring his specifications?" "He had to come at least once a year to report." Webster turned to the jury again. "He is a 'consulting engineer', gentlemen, a mere ornamental officer." Towlerton Leather was preparing to raise an objection to such a pointlessly offensive remark but

'If you cannot point
out a reason for the
embankment
breaking, we have
the right to assume
that it has failed
from bad
workmanship.'

John Webster

Webster carried on. "The specification was not a guide, it was a farce and a deception. I am completely out of patience!" That much, at least, was clear to everyone present,"I am not surprised at what has occurred and yet the Water Company will not admit to a single mistake. They assumed that everything had been perfect!" "Not perfect, maybe, but we did the best so far as our knowledge went," put in Gunson. "Then I am sorry that you have so little knowledge!" came the reply. Gunson shook his head, quite bewildered at the turn of events, "It is a great misfortune," he said, though quite which misfortune he referred to was not clear. Webster took a couple of paces and turned again on Gunson. Here, he felt, was the core of the problem and he was determined to push home his advantage. "These engineers," he said, pointing, "can say what they like but they had no right to depart from the specifications. They constructed the embankment quite contrary to the manner specified and then said that it was perfect. It will not do at all!" Webster was becoming so agitated that one of the jurymen, dismayed at the unorthodox manner of the proceedings, felt impelled to reproach him. "I think you should take it more deliberately, Mr. Coroner." "It is very hard to do so when the work has killed nearly three hundred of our fellow citizens," replied Webster, more calmly. "Mr. Smith. Have you any more witnesses?" "I think that Mr. Jackson has shown that the points questioning the workmanship of the dam were matters of doubt," replied Smith. "But if you cannot point to a reason for the embankment failing have we not a right to assume that it did so through bad workmanship?" "No, we still conjecture that it came about through a natural slip of the ground outside the bank. I assume that the jury entertain no idea of finding anyone criminally responsible so there can be little purpose in pursuing this inquiry further. I must say, on behalf of the Water Company, that they will continue to make every inquiry possible into the cause of the accident, and more maturely than we have seen here!"

Mr. Pawson, the foreman, approached the Coroner. The two spoke quietly and then the jury retired to consider the question of criminality. Maybe they were keen to finish the whole charade as soon as possible. For only twenty minutes later they filed back and Henry Pawson handed Webster a piece of paper. He read the note of the verdict and then took off his spectacles and turned slowly to the court. "The jury have come to a verdict in this matter, so it will be unnecessary for me to sum up. Perhaps this is as well, for I might have spoken more strongly than people would have liked! Gentlemen, would you please deliver your verdict?" Henry Pawson stood. "Certainly, Mr. Coroner. We find that Thomas Elston came to his death by drowning in the inundation caused by the bursting of the Bradfield dam on March 12th." Mr. Gunson involuntarily held his breath, anticipating the jury's condemnation of his work. "In our opinion, there has not been that engineering skill and attention in the construction of the works which their magnitude and importance demanded." The foreman's voice continued, saying something about ensuring better government inspection, but John Gunson heard none of it. "Lack of skill and attention" they had said. He could hardly believe it. He, whose every waking concern had been with detail and precision, would be on record for his 'lack of skill and attention'. He pulled on his coat and quietly, without speaking, walked from the Town Hall, up High Street, to his house on Division Street.

* * * * * * * * * * * * *

The result of this unsatisfactory inquest was quite the reverse of that intended by the impetuous Webster. The actual witnesses to the disaster had not been called to give evidence. The evidence of the engineers had been relied upon, and they had failed to ascribe a cause for the dam's collapse despite all the coroner's efforts. The sheer vagueness of the jury's verdict seemed to exonerate the Company from direct blame for the disaster. As March turned to April memories of the initial horror dimmed and, as the shattered town gradually began to get back to normal working, the national spotlight faded. Ordinary Sheffielders were dismayed by the prospect of the Water Company squirming out of their clear responsibility for the accident. When a group of eminent engineers appointed by the Company to carry out their own investigation into the disaster reported that they considered the pipes to have been laid in a correct manner and that no fault could be found with the building of the embankment this seemed ever more likely. Contrary to the opinion of Robert Rawlinson these engineers, probably not surprisingly, leaned towards Towlerton Leather's contention that the ground had slipped beneath the embankment. Few people in the town, however, including the Mayor, could have been cynical enough to have anticipated the Company's subsequent manoeuvring.

At the end of April the Water Company issued a report on the way that it intended to proceed. Whilst repudiating the generally held opinions of the cause of the failure of the embankment the Company could do little but accept general liability. Unfortunately, however, they would be unable to meet the claims from existing funds and intended to seek Parliamentary permission to raise new capital and to levy a moderate increase in the water rates. In return the Company pledged to provide a constant supply of water to the town within five years. The deal appeared reasonable enough, and even the Town Council were prepared to acquiesce, until it became known, in the details of the proposed Bill, that the modest increase which was being proposed was in fact twenty five percent! In effect the townsfolk were to be charged to pay the debts of the Company incurred as a result of the failure of its own dam. The Council was appalled and set about preparing its opposition to such an outrageous proposal. William Leng, in the pages of *The Telegraph,* reflected the view of most of Sheffield, that the waterworks should be taken over by the municipality as had occurred, with excellent results, in other towns. Opposition was drawn against the Company's Bill and it appeared to have little chance of success. Whilst the Company had insufficient funds to meet its obligations, however, it found enough to employ skilled and experienced lawyers to act on its behalf when the matter came before a Commons Select Committee and, unlikely as the result had appeared at the outset, the Act was passed, despite the fierce representations of the Council, and the twenty five percent increase was approved. To the ordinary Sheffielder it was yet again the victory of privilege and position.

CHILD'S WOODEN BATTLEDORE.

Kelham Island
Museum

The Act, which came into force at the end of July, also stipulated the framework for the hearing and agreement of the many claims for compensation which were rapidly mounting against the Company. It was not until the beginning of October, however, that the three man commission, under William Overend QC. took their places in the committee room at Sheffield Town Hall and began to sift through the six and a half thousand claims for destroyed and damaged property and the several hundred for death and injury. For the next six months the commissioners would be presented with a daily succession of petitioners representing a remarkable cross section of the town's population, from the poorest and most lowly to the wealthy and enterprising. Their stories were frequently pitiable and tragic in the extreme, sometimes dishonest and occasionally ludicrous, but the whole proceedings were painstakingly recorded in copperplate handwriting in twelve great black ledgers, now one of the greatest treasures of the Sheffield City Archives.

The one aspect of these records which strikes today as most unjust and harsh is the underlying assumption that property could be valued, but human life was judged to have a value only in terms of the loss of earning power. The manufacturing companies, therefore, tended to be fully reimbursed for their losses, but little compensation was awarded for the loss of relations unless they were the breadwinner. This appeared no less harsh at the time. The case of William Coggin, who had returned with his wife from a funeral in Wakefield to their cottage in Neepsend, was typical. "Mr. and Mrs. Coggin. Good afternoon", said William Overend as the couple advanced towards the bench. "Please tell us the nature of your claim." "We lost our three children in t'flood." "We are extremely sorry to hear that, Mr Coggin. Can you give us details of the children?" "Aye, there were our Alfred, aged thirteen, Eliza, she were nine, and little William, six." "And how much do you wish to claim for their deaths?" "We've been advised to claim £350, sir." "What income did the children earn?" "Well, Alfred, he were working for the skinners on Neepsend Lane. He earned eight shilling a week, but he often earned more doing odd jobs like." The commissioners consulted for a few moments before coming back to the Coggins. "In view of the fact that Alfred was working we are able to award you the sum of £25." "What?" shrieked the distraught mother, "Is that all for all our suffering? If that's all I can expect for the lives of my children I'll have a life for it!"

But the commissioners were constrained by the harsh limits of the Act which enabled them to grant nothing for personal grief and anguish. Poor Selina Dyson of Hillsbrough, who lost all seven of her family, was granted £60 of her claim for £500, and Mrs. Ryder, whose son Robert was swept away whilst clinging to his mother's skirt while she clung onto a lamppost, received £20, as he was earning 4s 6d a week. Paul Spooner, a boot maker from Neepsend Lane, was satisfied, however, with the £5 which he received for the loss of his fox terrier. William Howe, of Bacon Island, was granted a handsome £110 for the loss of furnishings which included the piano and music, wax fruit and flowers, 'The History of England' in four volumes and a mahogany card table. The destroyed stock of Joseph Appleton's stationery shop in Blonk Street, complete with its Valentines, was valued at £200 and that of Levi Fox, the toy dealer, at £110. Amongst the strangest items that compensation was claimed for must be the unsavoury materials of the tanneries at Neepsend which listed 292 tons of oak bark, 7 tons of valonia and 20 casks of dog manure.

There were, of course, a few rogues who seized the opportunity to make fraudulent claims. We only know about the ones, such as John Harris, nicknamed 'Bony', who were rumbled. Harris, a grinder who lived on Penistone Road, had claimed, and been awarded, £500 compensation in respect of a head injury sustained in the course of the flood. When new evidence in this matter was brought to the commissioners attention, they recalled him to the court. "Mr. Harris, could you please repeat to us the story which you told us about how you came to injure your head?" "Aye, it were on t'night of flood. I were sleeping on sofa downstairs when suddenly water rushes into t'house. I got up and I tried to run for t'stairs but water tipped t'sofa over and it cracked me on t'head. I'd have drowned fer sure if t'wife hadn't come downstairs and dragged me out." "Mr. Harris, you are a grinder by trade?" "Aye, I am." "Is it not the case that you have on several occasions been struck about the head by flying fragments of grindstones?" "Well, I can't really recall as I have." "Mr. Harris, we have received information that on one occasion your chin was cut and some of your teeth knocked out and that on another occasion a piece of a broken stone struck you in the face, breaking your nose. Is that correct?" "Aye, but I'd never done anything to t'back of my head before then." "Come now, Mr. Harris, you must have had an occasional bang on the head." "Well, I was once hit by an overhanging branch when I was travelling on the top of t'bus back from Buxton." "And did you receive any treatment for this injury?" "Aye, some hair got into t'wound and it wouldn't heal so old Mrs. Sylvester come round and put some leeches on it. It healed up right as rain after that." "And are there any other occasions when you have injured your head?" "Well, not so you'd notice, though there were once when I fell in t'Lancers on a piece of tobacco pipe." "Why is it, Mr. Harris, that you said nothing to you workmates about the accident that you had in the flood?" "I don't say nowt to them about my private affairs. There were once I said summat and t'next day they'd took my leather bands, because I'm not in t'union." "We have received information that on the night of the flood you actually went out to Bridge Street to check on your donkey." "I never did. I didn't see him till next day when they brought him to me and I gave him something warm to eat." "Thank you, Mr. Harris" said William Overend. "Can Mrs. Sylvester step forwards please?" An aged woman in a woollen shawl made her way to the give evidence. "Mrs Sylvester, did you treat Mr. Harris's head wound with leeches?" "I did." "Can you please take a look and tell us if the scar that you can see on his head is the same that you treated?" "It is, sir." "Thank you. Now can Mr. Mills stand forward? Mr. Mills, are you the barber who has cut Mr. Harris's hair on a number of occasions?" "I am sir, I've been cutting his hair for years." "And do you remember seeing the scar on the back of his head before the night of the flood?" "Oh, yes sir. He's had that scar for years!"

By early April of 1865 the proceedings were drawing to a close. The commissioners had patiently pronounced judgement on the thousands of claims and had awarded about £275,000 in damages, a sum considerably less than the company had expected. The Waterworks Company had got off lightly, and given the political climate of the day this was not so surprising. What is extraordinary is the fact that the Relief Committee, which had done such stalwart work in those first days following the disaster in collecting contributions, found themselves, almost two years later, in the embarrassing position faced by many such groups of having a considerable surplus left over. In fact some £30,000 of the original £55,000 still remained, and was returned to the donors or handed to local hospitals, so there had been little reason for the relief bodies to have been so harsh and mean-spirited towards those whose whole lives had been wrecked on the night of March 11th, 1864.

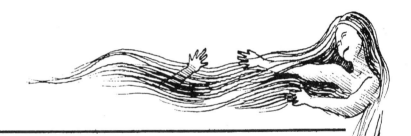

O man! how vain thy boasted skill, how feeble is thy power,

To him, who can the work of years, destroy in one short hour,

To thy ambition, Sheffield lays this elemental strife.

This wide expance of misery, and fearful waste of life!

But while a throb beats in thy heart, or mem'ry holds her throne,

God grant the like calamity, may ne'er again be known!

Last verse of "Lines Written on The Great Flood"

Echoes of the Past

It was, quite unrelatedly, in the same year as the flood that local by-laws were enacted forbidding the building of back-to-back courtyard dwellings, a vital indication of the way that things were changing. Sanitation was improved and, little by little, the living conditions of the poorest inhabitants of the Borough became more tolerable, although it was to be some time after Sheffield was conferred with the status of a city, in 1897, that the horrific infant mortality rate would fall significantly. Towards the end of the century the city's steel, engineering and cutlery industries boomed and the march of bricks and mortar proceeded faster than ever, the new horse-drawn trams speeding workers from Hillsbrough and beyond to the sprawling factories in the Don Valley and to the city centre shops and offices. It was an exciting time of growth and development. Sheffield had little inclination to hark back to stories which, although only thirty years old, already belonged to a past age. Together with the tales of Charlie Peace, the notorious murderer, and the memories of the outrages committed by the trades unions, the story of 'The Sheffield Flood' became simply a part of local folklore. Although there had been suggestions that it would be fitting to erect a public memorial to those who died in the flood it now seemed irrelevant and the proposal got no further.

In the midst of later urban redevelopments there are still a surprising number of survivals of buildings which feature in the story of the flood. Near the city centre the great railway viaduct still straddles The Wicker and the red-brick Royal Victoria Hotel, where Rowlinson stayed, still stands beside the now derelict station. Some of the pubs along the flood's route which served as receiving houses for bodies still do business. Some parts of the Workhouse still stand on Alma Street, opposite Kelham Island, as the building was incorporated into a steel works. Kelham Island itself is still occupied by engineering works as well as the city's industrial museum, which occupies the shell of the tramway's electrical generating station, and the view of the river from the island is evocative of the time of the flood. The rear of grimy cutlery and engineering factories still rise directly from the polluted water, protruding pipes still discharging suspicious looking effluent, but, looking up the river from the end of the island the view of James Dixon's factory, rising behind Ball Street Bridge, is magnificent. Despite a recent fire which seriously damaged the derelict building it is good to see that it is to be refurbished and given a new lease of life as up-market accommodation.

Further up, Bacon Island has long since disappeared beneath industrial developments but nearby The Farfield Inn still stands, virtually unaltered beside Hillfoot Bridge, which was rebuilt in stone. Above the confluence of the Don and the Loxley, Wardsend Cemetery still sprawls up the hill. There are said to be graves of flood victims here, marked with cast-iron headstones, but the graveyard is so abandoned and overgrown that I have never been able to find them. In Owlerton The Shakespeare and The Old Blue Ball still stand and both have recently had fixed to their walls plaques, produced by Hillsbrough Community Development Trust, to record their part in the story of the flood. The imposing bulk of the Barracks stands facing these across the river. Its original purpose having long ago been superceded, it served for many years as the unlikely premises for Burdall's Gravy factory before being transformed to accommodate modern retail outlets.

But it is the landscape of the Loxley Valley itself that today preserves most poignantly the faint echoes of the past. John Gunson would undoubtedly recognise much of the road up the Loxley Valley above Malin Bridge which he travelled that night on the eve of the flood, for this, the quietest of Sheffield's valleys, has been little affected by urban sprawl and has been surprisingly little developed. Water power held sway longer in this backwater, aided no doubt by the boost that the local manufacturers received from being able to entirely rebuild their mills with the compensation payments. They exhibited typical conservatism in rebuilding water wheels so late into the age of steam, and the valley is still dotted with the relics of these ventures. Mill ponds still bead the river's length and at Olive Wheels, Little Matlock and Malin Bridge fascinating industrial hamlets survive, their waterwheels still intact. There are far worse ways to spend a pleasant Sunday afternoon than to follow the footpaths beside the river from Malin Bridge up to Damflask.

The reservoirs which guaranteed the constant supply of water to turn the wheels were completed in the years following the disaster; Agden in 1869, Strines in 1871 and Dale Dyke, rebuilt a few hundred yards higher up the valley than the stricken dam, in 1875. The final reservoir, the Damflask, drowned the site of the little settlement of the same name which had been devastated by the flood. Stone farmsteads still dot the valley sides and the windswept settlement of High Bradfield still perches high above the valley, a tiny group of farms and cottages with its exquisite church surrounded by the graveyard in which the Tricketts still rest. Sheep graze the hillside right up to its railings and from this vantage point the sun can be seen glinting on the water of the Dale Dyke reservoir far below. Low Bradfield, at the bottom of the hill, has its own charm. The infant river runs through here, a favourite spot to bring the children for a picnic, to feed the local ducks and possibly have a paddle beside the bridge. But the village has never quite regained the vitality which was washed away in 1864 and today its centre is occupied by the cricket field. Joseph Ibbotson's cornmill was rebuilt and worked into the present century but burned down during the last war. The bridges and the Wesleyan Chapel were also rebuilt and still stand. The village school, however, closed some years ago. Today the frightful events of 1864 find few echoes in this rural backwater.

Of the site of the disaster surprisingly little can be seen today. A small memorial plaque, erected with donations from The Bradfield Historical Society in 1991, stands next to the footpath. It is possible to walk through the conifer plantations which now cover the area once occupied by the embankment but all that remains of it are a few humps and hollows. Across these, amongst the trees, the Water Company has erected a series of small, white, marker stones, each one marked C.L.O.B. These letters stand for the words 'Centre Line of Old Bank'. It always strikes me that this is a most enigmatic and inadequate memorial to those who lost their lives in a disaster of the scale and dramatic impact of that which occurred here all those years ago.

References

1. *A Complete History of the Great Flood at Sheffield,* Samuel Harrison. First published, S. Harrison, 1864. Reprinted on several occasions, most recently by Evans and Langley, with a foreword by Mary Walton, in 1974.

2. *The Collapse of the Dale Dyke Dam, 1864* Geoffrey Amey. Cassell & Co. 1974.

3. *The Illustrated London News,* March 19th 1864.

4. *The Illustrated London News,* March 26th 1864.

5. *The Star Flood Centenary Souvenir,* March 7th 1964.

6. *The Flood Claims, A Postscript to the Sheffield Flood,* Jean Cass.

7. *John Towlerton Leather and the Collapse of the Dale Dyke Dam,* G.M. Binnie, in *Early Water Engineers.*

8. *The Great Flood,* Supplement to the *Sheffield Daily Telegraph,* March 14th 1964.

9. *The Great Sheffield Flood, 1864, A collection of Lantern Slides and Accompanying Text,* E.G.Drape. Published by Hillsborough Community Development Trust 1995.

Relics of the Flood

A LITTLE DOLLS BASKET

Kelham Island Museum

James Dixons and
Ball street Bridge